"*The Nonprofiteer's Fundraising Field Guide* is a groundbreaking book. While many books have been written about servant-leadership in recent years, this is the first one written specifically for nonprofit professionals, and it is outstanding in all respects. Through his analysis of servant-leadership characteristics including listening, empathy, building a sense of community, and others, Evan Wildstein offers many compelling and practical tips for fundraisers, executives, board members, and others associated with non-profit organizations. This will be a must-have book for years to come."

—LARRY C. SPEARS, president and CEO,
The Spears Center for Servant-Leadership

"*The Nonprofiteer's Fundraising Field Guide* is a modern manifesto for the fundraiser ready to step into more alignment in their values, leadership, and impactful work. With his signature smart and witty guidance, Evan Wildstein unpacks ten principles of servant-leadership that leads to more connection, more community and (of course!) more fundraising success too. Whether you're a seasoned fundraiser or just getting started, keep this guide within an arm's reach to grab a boost of confidence and the encouragement to keep going."

—JON McCOY, co-founder and CEO, We Are for Good

"Evan Wildstein succinctly distills what it means to be an authentic servant leader in philanthropy in this refreshing new resource for the social sector. If you are feeling stuck and seeking direction in your nonprofit career, let this be the map that guides you out of the woods and towards fundraising success."

—RYAN GINARD, author of *Future Philanthropy*

"Evan Wildstein has written an inspiring and tactical book on how to become the sensitive, connected, and enlightened fundraisers we all strive to be. With actionable advice and real-life examples, this book should be on every leader's desk. If we know better, we do better, and Evan has provided a roadmap."

—RHEA WONG, author of *Get That Money, Honey!*

The Nonprofiteer's Fundraising Field Guide

The Nonprofiteer's Fundraising Field Guide

30 Practical Ways to Boost Philanthropy
Through Servant-Leadership

EVAN WILDSTEIN

RESOURCE *Publications* • Eugene, Oregon

THE NONPROFITEER'S FUNDRAISING FIELD GUIDE
30 Practical Ways to Boost Philanthropy Through Servant-Leadership

Resource Publications
An Imprint of Wipf and Stock Publishers
199 W. 8th Ave., Suite 3
Eugene, OR 97401

www.wipfandstock.com

PAPERBACK ISBN: 978-1-6667-6751-3
HARDCOVER ISBN: 978-1-6667-6752-0
EBOOK ISBN: 978-1-6667-6753-7

04/11/23

Contents

Introduction   1

Servant-Leadership: A Primer for Newbies   5

What About Servant-Leadership and Philanthropy?   11

Boosting Philanthropy Through Servant-Leadership   17

On Servant-Leadership and Diversity   58

You've Reached the End of the Beginning   62

The Long and Short of It   65

All My Immeasurable Gratitude   69

Appendix One: Donation Acknowledgement Communication
        Hierarchy   71

Appendix Two: Fundraising Stay Interview Questions   73

Bibliography   77

Introduction

WELCOME, NONPROFITEERS. I AM SO glad you are here. You've made the choice to crack open the pages of this bite-sized book. Congratulations. You *are* a nonprofiteer—someone who believes in social impact and knows the tremendous value our efforts add to our communities. You love being a champion for non-profit organizations and their people. Your bookshelves, inboxes, and web browser tabs are all (probably) filled with data, research, and articles on how to improve our sector, even if you haven't read them yet. (But you'll definitely get to them soon, right?) You likely attend workshops and listen to great podcasts. Maybe you've also pursued formal studies in nonprofit management, fundraising, operations, and beyond. And you do all this in the name of making nonprofits better.

This is difficult enough to do in normal times. These are not normal times. These are difficult, different times. Nearly every single day we experience great challenges and changes in front of us, beside us, and all around us. This isn't a new reality, but doesn't it feel like the pressure is consistently "on?" And yet, the more things change, the more things remain the same. Countless creatives have deliberated on this, like writer Jean-Baptiste Alphonse Karr, rock singer Bon Jovi, and others.

John Burkhardt and Larry Spears mused on this too in their concise book from the year 2000, *Servant-Leadership and Philanthropic Institutions*. They explained to us how philanthropy morphs and evolves in tandem with the world itself. Like Karr and Bon Jovi,

1

their sentiment was as true and relevant decades ago as it is today. Look around at the contemporary landscape of ever-evolving social concerns like global health crises, racial injustice, economic inequity, and countless other issues that disparage our communities. The social impact sector concerns itself with these issues, and it seeks to improve on them. Philanthropy is a big part of what makes it possible for these improvements to happen. Fundraising leaders pay close attention to those issues as they seek to bridge the space between donors and the world donors seek to change. And make no mistake, it is a delicate space. One that requires a great deal of care and attention—like a gardener who tends to their lot.

You don't need to look far to find others who explore these issues in the mainstream. (And if you're not familiar with these resources, please check them out.) Publications like *Chronicle of Philanthropy, Nonprofit Quarterly*, and *Philanthropy News Digest*. Professional organizations like CFRE International, Nonprofit Leadership Alliance, and Association of Fundraising Professionals. And even (especially) media podcasts—I lost count when scrolling through 250 of them on the internet.

But what *is* leadership in fundraising? When many people hear the word "leader" they think about an organization's hierarchy: the chief executive officer in the corner office (or corner cubicle) guiding it forward, or the boss who directs or manages an amalgam of processes, projects, and plans. When I first launched into my career in the early 2000s, that was my perspective too. But the concept is more nuanced than that.

In his compendium on the subject, *Leadership*, Peter Northouse provides what I believe is one of the best descriptions there is. "Leadership is a process whereby an individual influences a group of individuals to achieve a common goal."[1] Notice the words Northouse chose: process, influence, common goal. Then notice what is missing. Nowhere in the description does it say anything about a position, title, education, or years of experience. Yet often we believe a leader is someone in a certain role, with a certain designation,

---

1. Northouse, *Leadership*, 5.

with certain credentials, for a certain period of time. But through influence, most anyone, in any position, can *practice* leadership. Being influential means keeping an eye on the future. In the pages of this field guide, you will learn exactly how servant-leaders have a unique ability to look ahead. (There's more on this under "Foresight" on pages 38–42.)

One interesting story comes from Fons Trompenaars and Ed Voerman's *Servant-Leadership Across Cultures*. In it, they wrote about former Motorola CEO, Bob Galvin. When Galvin learned of an employee's glaring mistake that cost the company $100,000, he had the tough choice of firing the person or learning from the mishap. As a servant-leader, Galvin leaned in. He encouraged the worker to help Motorola learn how to avoid similar errors. The result? A report that helped save the company more than $1 million over time.

Leadership in fundraising can, and often does, play a similar role. Although Galvin was at the top of the ladder at Motorola, philanthropic leadership doesn't always translate to someone in a "chief" position. Philanthropy is about service to the greater good. (Even its etymological root translates to "love of mankind.") Although effective fundraising leadership *may* come from a nonprofit's CEO, it can come from a grants manager, board member, database administrator, and other staff or volunteers—truly anyone who *influences* funding by driving organizational missions forward.

This field guide was inspired by the many opportunities servant-leadership can provide to foster better philanthropy and a better nonprofit sector. As you read on, you'll soak up some knowledge on servant-leadership. You'll read a brief background on Robert Greenleaf, the man who gave servant-leadership its name. You'll also learn about several others who have directly (and indirectly) built on his legacy over the past half century.

I also want to be very clear about what you *won't* find in these pages. *The Nonprofiteer's Fundraising Field Guide* is not a deep digest on the topics of social impact, philanthropy, or servant-leadership. Those already exist, and many of them are quite wonderful. (I point to several of those resources throughout this book.)

3

Clocking in under 90 pages, this book is meant to inspire you swiftly. I have hopes you will keep it on your desk, in your bag, and around you often. That you'll use it as a resource to grow more functional and inspired fundraising teams, build deeper relationships with donors, and increase philanthropic dollars for your organizations. You might dog-ear the pages, make notes in the margins, cover it with Post-its, and snap photos of different parts to share with your colleagues and teams. If you do all that, I will consider it a great compliment.

In his essay, *The Institution as Servant*, Greenleaf wrote: "Trust is first. Nothing will move until trust is firm."[2] It is my goal for these pages to demonstrate the practical value of servant-leadership in such a way that fundraisers—and our entire social impact industry—will *trust* in the philosophy's capacity to move, and improve, philanthropy.

Thanks again, nonprofiteers. I am very glad you are here.

2. Greenleaf, *Servant Leadership*, 101.

Servant-Leadership:
A Primer for Newbies

"THE SERVANT-LEADER *IS* SERVANT-FIRST. . . . That person is sharply different from one who is *leader* first."[1] Robert Greenleaf penned these words more than fifty years ago. They come from his seminal essay that launched servant-leadership into the fore, *The Servant as Leader*.

For those unfamiliar with the movement Greenleaf inspired, a number of examples will be found in the following pages. But we are nonprofiteers who are all about relationships, aren't we? In that way, to understand what servant-leadership *is*, it may help to reflect on *who* servant-leaders are (or were) as people. Throughout history, we have examples of those whose lives embodied the philosophy. People like Abraham Lincoln, Martin Luther King Jr., Mother Teresa, and even polymath Albert Schweitzer. All were extraordinary individuals who could have taken actions that were short-term and self-serving. Instead, they led extraordinary lives through service with the greater good in mind.

Greenleaf crystallized his notion for servant-leadership in the late 1950s after reading Hermann Hesse's book, *Journey to the East*. At the time, Greenleaf was nearing retirement after a long career with AT&T—a very different company than the telecom giant we now know in the twenty-first century. He would then launch a very successful second wind during which he counseled for-profit

1. Greenleaf, *Servant Leadership*, 27.

and not-for-profit organizations alike. In Hesse's pages, he found a muse: Leo, a servant who, by the end of the story, presents as being the most important character. Greenleaf said,

> In this story we see a band of men on a mythical journey, probably also Hesse's own journey. The central figure of the story is Leo who accompanies the party as the *servant* who does their menial chores, but who also sustains them with his spirit and his song. He is a person of extraordinary presence. All goes well until Leo disappears. Then the group falls into disarray and the journey is abandoned. They cannot make it without the servant Leo.[2]

Greenleaf's overall thesis was profound yet wildly simple, as John Burkhardt and Larry Spears suggested in *Servant-Leadership and Philanthropic Institutions*: "True leadership emerges from those whose primary motivation is a deep desire to help others."[3] (Remember this line for later.)

Early on I also want to address something you may find curious: the hyphen between the words *servant* and *leader*. I used to think it seemed strange or at least grammatically incorrect, and others have pondered this too. Servant-leader expert Pat Falotico addressed it this way,

> The servant, without the leader, is focused on providing for others. . . . The leader, without the servant, is focused on achieving goals, fulfilling the mission he or she has been charged with and growing their sphere of influence. . . . The servant-leader is more than the "and" of these two nouns. Servant-leaders humbly accept that they achieve goals when they help their team members achieve their highest aspiration and connect them to a compelling purpose. Their focus is lifting the capacity of others, with no expectation of what they get in return. It is the richest way to live and find meaning.[4]

---

2. Greenleaf, *Servant Leadership*, 21.

3. Burkhardt and Spears, *Servant-Leadership*, 3

4. Falotico, "Servant-Leader: Why the Dash?"

Falotico's words suggest a spirit of collaboration. If there is an assumed relationship between *servant* and *leader*—within someone who claims or strives to be a servant-leader—there should also be a connection with the followers that person intends to lead. In so much of Greenleaf's writing he explores this two-way relationship between leaders and followers, along with the power dynamics that exist between them. But he certainly wasn't the first. Others have long theorized the ways that businesses can be the tides that lift everyone involved.

Nearly one-half century before Greenleaf, organizational theorist Mary Parker Follett explored the subject in her 1924 treatise, *Creative Experience*. Follett wrote that the only growable power is *genuine power*. She posited that genuine power is coactive rather than coercive, saying, "Coercive power is the curse of the universe; *coactive* power, the enrichment and advancement of every human soul."[5] (Italics mine.)

But what about the time before, between, and after Follett and Greenleaf? What prevented a public surge in the ideals of helping others, and enriching and advancing human souls (as Follett pondered)?

"In the 1950s and 1960s," Harvard's Barbara Kellerman wrote, "leaders were generally thought of as being commanding and controlling."[6] This mimics some of the "great man" characteristics we typically attribute to the world's quintessential business leaders. Traits like self-confidence, sociability, and determination. Kellerman further acknowledged that things began to slowly change near the late 1950s, suggesting "The idea that leaders could simply command and control and their will would be done gave way to the slow, sober realization that times were changing."

In 2011, columnist David Brooks reflected on this as well, contemplating,

> I wonder if sometime around 50 years ago a great mental tide began to sweep across the world. Before the tide, people saw themselves in certain fixed places in the social order. They accepted opinions from trusted authorities.

5. Follett, *Creative Experience*, xii.
6. Kellerman, *The End of Leadership*, 27–28.

7

As the tide swept through, they began to see themselves differently. They felt they should express their own views, and these views deserved respect.[7]

With all these big pivots, one might have expected a philosophy like servant-leadership to thrive. After all, it has all the right ingredients for a delightful leadership stew. However, the growth was, and continues to be, slow. This is especially true when compared to other contemporaries in the leadership space. For example, Amazon's list of top books on leadership features familiar names. People like Stephen Covey, Brené Brown, Jim Collins, Simon Sinek, and others. All organizational titans whom Greenleaf inspired.

But what about Greenleaf himself? He rarely, if ever, appears on any such list.

One reason may be the words Greenleaf chose for his philosophy. In their very practical book, *Seven Pillars of Servant Leadership*, James Sipe and Don Frick pondered, "Does anyone *really* want to be a servant?"[8] They wondered about the possibility of preserving strong financial performance (remember this for later too) while leading and serving people.

Beyond the words alone, the phrase "servant-leader" suggests some paradoxes. We tend to assign leadership theories, traits, and archetypes a sense of being monolithic, as if everything were viewed through an identical prism. Greenleaf wrote deeply about attributes like *listening* and *empathy* and *building community* and more. But very few have pointed to concrete ways to activate these servant-leader ideals within and throughout an organization. Even fewer have explored this within the bounds of nonprofit life. In *Servant-Leaders in Training*, John Henry Horsman acknowledged all the various writing and research available on the topic. Yet he deliberated, "It remains difficult to put a circle around Servant-leadership and say *this is what it is*—there always seems to be more to it."[9]

Although it can be difficult to clearly describe servant-leadership, one story from Paul Davis and Larry Spears's *Fortuitous*

7. Brooks, "The Quest for Dignity."

8. Sipe and Frick, *Seven Pillars*, 1.

9. Horsman, *Servant-Leaders in Training*, xi.

Encounters does the job incredibly well. (At under 100 pages, their book is like *Chicken Soup for the Servant-Leader Soul*.) In one specific experience, Davis recalled a small dinner with Coretta Scott King, the wife of Martin Luther King Jr. Davis learned the Kings chose not to have carpet in their home because the people who looked up to them considered carpet a luxury. King said, "I don't have carpet because I choose to lead poor people."[10]

Davis's takeaway from the conversation was simple and incredibly effective: "During that fortuitous encounter, I learned that leadership is not about what you get by being a leader, but about what you are willing to give up."[11] I vividly remember placing my bookmark between the pages, putting down the book, and staring out the window for what felt like an eternity. At the time it challenged nearly everything I had come to believe about the relationship between bosses and employees. As your guide on this servant-leadership journey, let me explain why.

In my pre-social impact days, I spent many years as a rock 'n' roll singer. When I left music to become a nonprofiteer, I did not veer far from the path and chose to produce artistic performances and other creative programs for different nonprofits. Between my rock music past and early career, I had spent nearly two decades "in the spotlight." If you're into personality assessments, I'm an enneagram type eight: the challenger. My type is known to be self-confident, willful, and confrontational. Being in front of the curtain came naturally.

If I were reading about the version of myself described here, I would think that person is a far cry from being a servant-leader. But guess who was a servant-leader *and* an enneagram eight? Martin Luther King Jr. Because enneagram eights are also honorable, and rabid protectors and champions of other people. Davis's story showed me I had something meaningful in common with people like the Kings. I began to lean into servant-leadership and learn how I could practice it in my professional life as a nonprofiteer. And *especially* as a fundraiser.

---

10. Davis and Spears, *Fortuitous Encounters*, 6.

11. Davis and Spears, *Fortuitous Encounters*, 6.

One thing I began doing immediately was refashioning recurring meetings with fundraisers on my team by turning the reigns over to them. This gesture of giving something up, by having teammates craft agendas and run the conversations, was challenging but also hugely transformational, for me *and* them. We started focusing less on routine updates and more on the big picture, discussing big accomplishments, upcoming priorities, roadblocks, and even quirky news. Over time their abilities began to grow, which resulted in learning and promotions for them. It also built better relationships with donors and increased revenue for our organization.

As with many servant-leader attributes, these small acts have big implications. This is great for any industry, especially philanthropy. Let's go deeper so you can see how it's all interconnected.

What About Servant-Leadership and Philanthropy?

EVEN IF THE PHRASE "servant-leadership" is new to you, it might feel like the philosophy's innate characteristics are ideal, if not commonplace, in nonprofits. I have found this to be true especially within the context of philanthropy. Yet, as a fundraiser, servant-leadership is not broadly discussed, and many of the same challenges noted earlier may explain why. There is also a serious gap in the existing literature and public discourse on the subject.

In the early 1970s, Greenleaf wrote two powerful articles focused on the donor perspective of philanthropy, "Foundation Trustees" and "Prudence and Creativity: A Trustee Responsibility." Framing these articles, he said plainly, "The most difficult way to serve may be the giving away of money."[1] His essays acknowledged the great challenges faced by humanity and how donors (especially institutions like foundations) can rise to meet these challenges. In doing so he addressed the consequential role funders play in raising what he called "the quality of the whole of American society."[2]

But while his writings were intriguing, Greenleaf offered mostly subjective, broadly interpretable suggestions about how servant-leadership can transform philanthropy. John Burkhardt and Larry Spears's dynamic essay (referenced earlier) approached servant-leadership and philanthropy in a similar way. To be clear,

1. Greenleaf, *Servant Leadership*, 215.
2. Greenleaf, *Servant Leadership*, 215.

their essay was a major inspiration for this entire field guide. Yet it also encouraged a much deeper dive into how one can realistically activate servant-leadership as a donor.

Opposite giving money away is the other side of the fence: fund-*raising*, or asking people, businesses, and other organizations to make monetary gifts. There are very few practical or academic fundraising resources supported by servant-leadership, but there should be. After all, there are more fundraisers in the US (more than 100,000) than there are baseball players, chiropractors, and economists combined![3]

As fundraisers we tend to focus our efforts on the entirety of the fundraising cycle. This includes the most common steps associated with philanthropy work: identification, qualification, cultivation, solicitation, and stewardship of donors.[4] However, to James Sipe and Don Frick's earlier point about financial performance, we must (or at the very least should) acknowledge that one of the primary functions of a fundraiser is to raise the highest possible amount of net revenue. Many among us believe in our duty of care and concern for donors. But at the end of the day, if we are not supporting our organizations by bringing robust revenue to the fore, our roles can become difficult to justify.

This is important, because even though our sector continues to generate more and more annual revenue—over $480 billion in 2021 and climbing[5]—charitable giving has languished at roughly 2.2 percent of US gross national product for half a century.[6] What's more, there is a measurable, growing gap in how many individuals donate directly to charity each year. In 2021 that figure was 56 percent, down from 65 percent in 2019.[7] This decline may be the result of many things. In the US specifically, the 2017 Tax Cut and Jobs Act brought consequential changes to charitable giving. It lowered individual income tax rates, increased standard deductions, and a

---

3. Bureau of Labor Statistics, "Occupational Outlook."
4. Haddad, "What is the Fundraising Cycle?"
5. Lilly Family School, "Giving USA."
6. National Association of Nonprofit Organizations, "The Nonprofit Sector."
7. Papandrea, "56% of Americans."

slew of other adjustments that disincentivized donors from giving for tax benefits.[8]

Donors are also finding different, novel ways to support causes with their dollars, such as crowdfunding vehicles like Kickstarter and GoFundMe, or nonprofit microfinance lenders like Kiva and Zidisha. And we can't forget about the growing gaggle of for-profit businesses that are changing the way individuals and institutions spend (or give away) their money. Several of them reinvest products or cash (or both) into high-need, well-deserving communities based on consumer sales. Some you've likely heard of, like footwear purveyors Bombas and TOMS. Some lesser-known companies include bracelet maker 4Ocean, ladies period underwear pioneer Thinx, and sustainable everyday item creator Mable.

But one thing is certain, as you read at the very beginning of this field guide: philanthropy is changing. (If this topic piques your interest, grab a copy of *The Generosity Crisis*, a brilliant book on the decline of donations by Nathan Chappell and Brian Crimmins.)

In this reality, fundraising can be laborious, and sometimes even downright exhausting. Beyond the vital task of generating revenue, we have donor visit summaries to upload in our databases, thank-you notes to write, staff meetings to attend, and countless other perpetual tasks. The work of a fundraiser never really ends. Acknowledging all this, exploring idealistic leadership constructs and approaches does not always rise to the level of concern for nonprofit professionals. However, thankfully, some of this homework has been done for us.

An enlightening report from four powerhouse social impact resource groups found that servant-leadership has the capacity to cultivate what we often call a "culture of philanthropy" in nonprofits. The direct result? Better organizations! "Servant leaders are increasingly seen as individuals who steward the talents and human resources of their organizations," the report authors noted. "The development of organizational systems and exchanges that foster the

---

8. Tax Policy Center, "How Did the TCJA."

stewardship of supporters is at the heart of what it means to have a truly philanthropic culture."[9]

Much the same was found with our friends in the corporate world. Other research has demonstrated that servant-led companies like The Container Store, Starbucks, and Southwest Airlines have average financial returns of 24.2 percent. (Although the latter two's servant-leadership resolve will be measured through the test of time, given some customer service letdowns from the early 2020s.) That's compared with other top, publicly traded companies whose returns average 10.8 percent.[10]

Wrapping together all these collective realities—and acknowledging that there is great potential for servant-leadership—I created this field guide with one simple hypothesis in mind: servant-leadership can boost fundraising for the betterment of nonprofits and their people.

To dive into this premise required a thorough review of all the research and literature available from thought leaders in the field. These popular experts advise that the best fundraisers possess certain skills, like being an exemplary listener, the capacity for storytelling, excellent communication, having situational awareness, and genuine interest in people.[11][12][13][14] However, I have never met those experts, and likely never will. It was equally important to invite feedback from my fellow nonprofiteers whose jobs directly (and indirectly) relate to philanthropy.

I created and shared a survey with my expanded network about organizational and fundraiser abilities. Responses came from a relatively small sample group of roughly 100 people. The survey began with the question: "What are the top three qualities you believe a fundraiser should possess to be successful?" Participants self-reported as being frontline fundraisers, gift administrators,

9. Concord Leadership Group, "the Wakeup Call."

10. Sipe and Frick, *Seven Pillars*, 2.

11. Lysakowski, "Top 10 Qualities."

12. McClaren, "5 Essential Traits."

13. Pun, "6 Key Skills."

14. Waltner-Pepper, "10 Core Personality Traits."

communications professionals, philanthropists, and program officers. Their responses mirrored the skills mentioned earlier. They also mirrored some of the characteristics most commonly associated with servant-leadership, as categorized by Larry Spears: listening, empathy, healing, awareness, foresight, conceptualization, stewardship, commitment to the growth of people, and building community.[15] The top answers were *awareness, building community, listening,* and *empathy,* collectively totaling 42 percent of responses.

Another question asked respondents to reflect personally, inquiring: "What are the top three qualities *you* bring to the field of philanthropy?" The answers were similar to the first question. *Building community* and *conceptualization* were the top servant-leader responses. (Coincidentally, also totaling 42 percent of responses.)

There was, however, one core servant-leader characteristic missing from the responses to both questions: persuasion. On persuasion, John Burkhardt and Larry Spears wrote, "Servant-leaders seek to convince others, rather than coercing compliance."[16] I have often heard fundraisers talk about their work in this way. They might say it is their responsibility to *convince* donors to make gifts. However, in a survey where comments were completely anonymous, it was interesting that not a single response related to the idea of needing to convince donors. Although this was surprising, it was heartening to know people fundamentally believe the best elements of fundraising are in lockstep with servant-leadership. Elements that build and grow—even if, ironically, they did not realize those are inherently servant-leader qualities.

Remember Burkhardt and Spears's earlier idea of *a deep desire to help others*? A final question in my survey asked about participants' familiarity with the philosophy of servant-leadership. Of the responses shared, there was an overwhelming belief that servant-leadership was about one thing: putting other people first. However, even though the question was open-ended, not a single clarifying statement was offered about *how* servant-leaders put others first, or to what end. This demonstrated another reason why the practice

15. Spears, "Character and Servant Leadership."
16. Burkhardt and Spears, *Servant-Leadership*, 4.

of servant-leadership may not be a common conversation topic in philanthropy, and that more exploration and literature are needed. Spears's core servant-leader characteristics were the baseline for this field guide because of his unique expertise. Not only was he the former president/CEO of the Greenleaf Center for Servant Leadership, he did the mammoth work of distilling Greenleaf's myriad writings into the tailored set of ten traits that underpin the quintessential servant-leader.[17] (He was also one of my most inspiring professors from graduate school.)

The list again, as Spears wrote, and where you can find them in this field guide, is as follows:

- *Listening* (pages 18–22)

- *Empathy* (pages 22–26)

- *Healing* (pages 26–30)

- *Persuasion* (pages 30–34)

- *Awareness* (pages 34–38)

- *Foresight* (pages 38–42)

- *Conceptualization* (pages 42–47)

- *Stewardship* (pages 47–50)

- *Commitment to the Growth of People* (pages 50–54)

- *Building Community* (pages 54–57)

17. Spears, "Character and Servant Leadership."

Boosting Philanthropy Through Servant-Leadership

NOW THAT YOU'RE A servant-leadership connoisseur, it's time to dive into the good stuff. What follows is an exploration of the ten core characteristics of servant-leadership. Each features three actionable ways to lean into, and grow, philanthropy. Some of the recommendations look inward at organizations' fundraising staff and leadership. Others directly address how to engage—and engage better—with donors.

To ground the characteristics further, you'll find short, moving tales from experts and enthusiasts in the field. These show how impactful servant-leadership can be when acted out. (You'll find these clearly marked with "STORY" tags.) Speaking with these fundraisers, coaches, consultants, artists, and others was some of the most meaningful work I've ever done.

The result of all this is to grow as fundraisers, grow revenue, and grow our organizations.

Before you begin this journey, I want to clarify one important point. I believe fundraising is the responsibility of everyone in a nonprofit. Maybe not *all the time*, but generating revenue is something every single staffer supports in their day-to-day work. To that end, don't misunderstand my use of the phrase "fundraiser" throughout this field guide. At their heart, these recommendations can apply to *all* colleagues in all organizations. CEOs, heads of fundraising, grants managers, board volunteers, and beyond.

Because, once more for good measure, *leadership is for everyone.*
Okay. Let's get this journey started.

LISTENING

"It begins with listening. . . . leaders have a special responsibility to remain attentive to the voice of those they serve."[1] In all corners of nonprofit life, we see evidence of leaders who lean into their work with a *do-something* attitude. They believe their responsibility is to solve problems directly. When it comes to fundraising, however, the simple art of listening is a profound opportunity we can offer to donors and other strategic partners. It's as Dr. Kent Keith posed,

> How can you meet people's needs if you don't know what their needs are? And how will you know, if you don't ask and listen? Listening is how servant-leaders connect with those they wish to serve, and learn what they need to know in order to serve them well.[2]

As a baseline, it helps to differentiate between hearing and listening as practices. The former is an automatic exercise in aural reception of sound, a physical act. The latter is a voluntary, mental absorption of what is being said.[3] Both involve our ears, but only one is guided by the mind. Too often we experience friends, family members, and colleagues who barely hear, let alone listen. Greenleaf claimed bias on this, noting, "Only a true natural servant automatically responds to any problem by listening *first*. . . . It is because true listening builds strength in other people."[4] One of the most meaningful gifts we can provide donors—and, frankly, all peers in our nonprofit orbits—is our ability to not simply hear them but to *listen* to them. "You cannot truly listen to anyone and do anything else at the same time," said M. Scott Peck in *The Road Less Traveled.*

1. Burkhardt and Spears, *Servant-Leadership*, 6.
2. Frick, *Greenleaf and Servant-Leader Listening*, Foreword.
3. Fuller, "The Difference Between Hearing and Listening."
4. Greenleaf, *Servant Leadership*, 30.

"If you are not willing to put aside everything. . . then you are not willing to truly listen."[5]

In many exchanges, listening is a more powerful act than speaking. Think of it this way: we can listen to roughly three times as many words as we can speak.[6] Perhaps it's really no surprise we have two ears but only one mouth.

I would venture to guess that many (if not most) nonprofiteers agree listening is a noble act. But how do we activate on this idea? Greenleaf gave us a suggested starting point: silence. He asked, "In saying what I have in mind will I really improve on the silence?"[7] Leaning into silence can be done in several ways.

- First thing's first, speak second. "When in a meeting, don't be one of the first to give a comment. . . . Hearing other people speak gives you a better sense of what to say and when to say it," expressed communications expert Steve Boyd.[8] This might be uncomfortable for those used to being early responders in conversations. (This has often been a challenge for me.) However, the technique is simple yet wise, and can lead to gleaning good information from donors by giving them a chance to contribute first.

  You can support this practice by trying, if possible, to speak only 25 percent of the time, leaving 75 percent to silently, and actively, listen. This can be hard math to determine in real-time. But if you find yourself stumbling over a donor's words or cutting them off, chances are you are *not* leaning into silence. When you do find that silent space you may discover some amazing things. But be prepared to receive ulterior news, like learning a donor is *not* interested in your organization or programs, or that their passions currently align with another organization entirely. (Bonus: If you happen to learn that a donor's interests might connect with another nonprofit, consider directing them to that organization. You'll read a

5. Peck, *The Road Less Traveled*, 125.
6. Baurain, "Teaching, Listening, and Generative Silence."
7. Greenleaf, *Servant Leadership*, 30.
8. Boyd, "The Beginning of Silence."

bit more about this, later, under "Building Community" on pages 54–57.)

STORY: Silent Listening and Respect Are Great Bedfellows
Leadership and fundraising coach Marc Pitman shared a cathartic listening story with me about a donor we'll call "Gabi." Gabi, an alumna of a school, had been making an annual five-figure gift in support of a specific department. When a particular faculty member from the department left the school, Gabi was upset. She reached out to Marc demanding her gift be returned. Marc was part of a leadership team that made a bold move by deciding to listen to Gabi's needs and return the funds. More than that, they also decided not to stop treating her with respect and dignity—after all, Gabi was an alum of the school before she was a donor. Following this experience, Marc spent more time listening to Gabi, and even invited her advice and guidance on another project unrelated to the school. Later, when the school was in the midst of leading a capital campaign, Gabi made a $500,000 commitment, citing the fact that she felt listened to by those entrusted with her care as a donor.

- When you feel like making a comment, pause. Fundraisers are some of the best communicators in social impact—they have to be! However, they don't always allow appropriate space in their conversations. This is especially true when asking for donations. The question, "Would you consider a gift of $10,000?" is often quickly followed by an interjection. Something like, "I know this is a lot of money, and if you can't do that much, I completely understand." Instead, before jumping to a conclusion for a donor, wait a few beats before you chime in. Four or five seconds may feel like an eternity, but in the grand scheme, you may allow the necessary, good space to learn what a donor really thinks—and to demonstrate you really care.

Test this out by recording yourself asking the $10,000 question above, and then let five actual seconds pass. Wait a few minutes and then rewatch the video. You'll see those five seconds aren't the eternity you originally felt.

The art of listening can extend beyond meetings and real-time conversations. When I was growing up in the 1980s, I vividly recall different types of stores would have suggestion boxes by the checkout counters. Customers would leave comments about any number of things, like requesting certain items or even adjusting their hours to accommodate different schedules. In response, store owners and staff would read the feedback and respond or improve. If you're a fan of the show *Ted Lasso*, you know the main character put such a box in his team's locker room. More than simply inviting the comments, Lasso acted on the suggestions. (Remember the shower water pressure?) We have the same opportunities in our nonprofit organizations, and it doesn't necessarily have to mean an actual, physical box.

- On your website, donation check-out page, or even in the footers of e-newsletters, consider opening up to communication. Link to an anonymous Google Form where you can invite stakeholders to share feedback about some element of your nonprofit's work. In fundraising especially, being open to constructive comments from donors can be a huge learning opportunity for those responsible for fundraising. But like Ted Lasso, you must make sure you (reasonably) act on the suggestions. You risk eroding trust if such feedback is made into the void. The new media company, We Are For Good, serves the social impact sector, and they take this approach seriously with online voicemails. Using an app called SpeakPipe, they accept recorded messages (anonymous if desired) on topics and suggestions for their business.

Let's circle back about that...

- Avoid steamrolling your conversational counterparts, and try to make sure you allow them more space to speak than you.

- Allow that space by leaning into silence. Four or five seconds of quiet can be transformational.

- Create multiple opportunities to listen to your donors by wrapping in technology.

EMPATHY

When I first began speaking openly about *The Nonprofiteer's Fundraising Field Guide*, a friend shared with me an interesting perspective. She humored me, listened patiently, and acknowledged that servant-leadership sounded interesting. By the end of our conversation, she asked me a pointed question: "As a sector, haven't we moved *beyond* servant-leadership? Shouldn't we be talking more about *empathy-based* leadership?"

My immediate reaction was a great big smile, because I knew two things.

First, I knew that to believe in and practice servant-leadership requires a constant, consistent desire to observe people and learn what makes them tick. (Sounds a little bit like fundraising, doesn't it?) In this way, there cannot be a conversation about servant-leadership that excludes the idea of empathy. Second, I knew it meant there really *was* a big opportunity for this book, because I witnessed, in real-time, the challenges with public perception and understanding about servant-leadership. This work began by pondering and researching some basics about empathy.

Most of the widely accepted definitions of empathy I've come across focus on the idea of putting ourselves in another person's shoes or feeling things as others might feel them. The word itself stems from the Greek *empatheia*, which translates to "in feeling." In his book, *Tell Me More About That*, empathy activist Rob Volpe points at two types of empathy: affective and cognitive. The former denotes our capacity to feel others' emotions, while the latter is more about taking their perspective. According to Volpe, the one we need to improve on is cognitive empathy, and he suggests five actionable steps to become empathetic: dismantling judgment; asking good questions; actively listening; integrating into understanding; and using solution imagination.

As a practical exercise for fundraisers, the first step of dismantling judgment may be the most direct route toward growing an empathetic relationship with our donors. This is important if for no other reason than it forces us to think about the myriad biases we, as nonprofiteers, bring to our work. Sometimes these biases are inherent and baked in. Other times they are the result of previous, lackluster experiences. And perhaps you're saying to yourself: *That's not me. I never let my past create biases that impact my future behaviors.* If so, that's okay. This is a safe space, and you can be honest! And when you're finally being honest, read on.

- "Judgment is like a brick wall we can't see past. . . . made up of stereotypes, assumptions, and biases often from past experiences," Volpe said.[9] It would not be difficult for a fundraiser to recall a poor experience with a funder. Maybe it was an unusually demeaning or condescending conversation with a family foundation's program officer, or an unnecessarily dismissive attitude from a corporate executive's assistant. Would it be fair to assume that every other foundation's program officer or corporate assistant will behave the same way? Definitely not. I refuse to believe most people wake up in the morning and think about how to make our lives more challenging. Yet, we all have some experience with this type of bias.

  In every new or renewed interaction with a donor, consider *dismantling judgments* that are based on things that may have happened in your past. I have a little personal hack to help with this. Before any meetings or conversation I expect might be particularly difficult, I jot the following line on a piece of scrap paper and then rip it up and throw it away: "I mean well, they mean well, this will be swell." (Practices like this can seem cheesy, but there's something rather useful and cathartic about tearing up a piece of paper.)

In *Servant-Leaders in Training*, John Henry Horsman presents an interesting, almost poetic take on empathy. He suggests it is a "*there I am also* perspective. . . . A *there I am also* perspective is more

9. Volpe, "5 Ways to Put Empathy to Work."

inclusive and empathetic than *me, myself, and I*."[10] This suggests a sense of being *with* another person in various contexts—like being present with, and connected to, them. This connection is such an important capability in our fast-paced, distracted world. Sometimes in fundraising our work is about empathetically (and physically) bringing other people along on a collective journey. A journey that should actively involve the peers we work alongside in our organizations.

- There is great benefit to including those who do "the work"— managers, board volunteers, faculty members, program directors—in meetings with donors. This demonstrates to our donors how critical the actual programming is to the organization and the communities we serve. Psychologist Carl Rogers wrote in *A Way of Being*, "For empathy, presence must precede practice."[11] We want to invite those colleagues to be present with us and encourage in them a *there I am also* perspective. Before you bring people along, however, make sure you prepare them for those meetings by providing a brief overview of the donor or prospect. Let them know if these individuals have a history with the organization or if the conversation will be new and exploratory. Also be sure to focus expectations so your partners know what to say, how to say it, and when.

STORY: How Can We Be Most Useful?
Steve, the CEO of one of Texas's large social service nonprofits, subscribes to many servant-leader ideals. In a joyfully winding conversation, he spoke openly with me about empathy in the way John Henry Horsman did—the perspective of being *there I am also*. Steve told the story of "Sandra." Sandra had made a transformational, seven-figure gift to another nonprofit and told Steve, in no uncertain terms, "I like what you do, but your organization won't ever receive that much from me." Yet Steve was undeterred, because he was truly interested in learning about Sandra, her interests, and the good she does for her community. What began with a simple question, "How can we be most useful for you?"

10. Horsman, *Servant-Leaders in Training*, 93.

11. Rogers, *A Way of Being*, 142.

led to quarterly coffees and Steve being an advocate for Sandra's passion: senior citizens. He even accompanied her to city council meetings in support of opening a new senior center. And wouldn't you know it? After being *there also*, Steve's nonprofit also was honored with a seven-figure gift from Sandra.

Although presence is important in connecting with donors, empathy can also be very much about the *practice* of what we do. We can't empathize if we don't try, and although this sounds simple, truly understanding another's perspective takes serious effort. In meetings with donors, lean in—figuratively and literally.

- This should go without saying, but remove distractions like cellphones and smartwatches, and be physically involved. Sit directly facing the person with whom you're in a conversation, and don't close your body language by crossing your arms or hunching over. In graduate school my professor, communications expert David Givens, told me, "More than 90 percent of face-to-face emotional communication is nonverbal." This takes practice, especially for those whose posture is not typically so open. It sounds silly, but rehearse this by sitting in front of a mirror and reciting the lyrics to one of your favorite songs—ones you don't need to think about—so you can focus wholly on how your body language appears. Like the *listening* recommendation earlier, you can also record yourself doing this to watch later.

Let's circle back about that...

- Look forward with fresh eyes by not assuming people in your future will behave like everyone from your past.
- Our colleagues sometimes know better than us. Bring them along to help share the full story.
- Free your mind and open your body language to welcome people into your conversation.

HEALING

Health isn't purely a physiological matter. Although this has been a more profound realization of the years since 2020, issues of organizational health (especially) predate pandemic times. In 2019 the World Health Organization added *burnout* to its list of "occupational phenomenon."[12] That same year, Texas A&M's Anthony Klotz began writing about what would later be dubbed "the great resignation."[13] That said, I've been proud of the nonprofit sector for finally moving issues of self-care, self-growth, and psychological safety from the bibliography to the table of contents (as it were). We haven't solved for it yet, but the conversations have begun in earnest. We are talking about how mental, emotional, and social well-being are as important to our overall health as the health of our bodies. In *Servant-Leaders in Training*, John Henry Horsman wrote that "healing is about being present and available enough to let go of the old. . . and become open to what may come, or what is emerging."[14] Especially in these difficult and turbulent times, we must give attention and care if we are to be present, available, and ready for the future.

Think about any conversation you led with a donor when, for whatever reason, emotions were high. Maybe the stress was on your end, or perhaps the donor was dealing with an unwell family member. Or maybe their company was going through a series of layoffs or restructuring. These are not difficult to imagine in the past few years. To aid in healing, did you immediately launch into your organization's needs? Or did you allow space to be *present and available*, like Horsman wrote?

In her book, *Listening: The Forgotten Skill,* human behaviorist Madelyn Burley-Allen gives some advice. She argues that we help people bring down emotional levels simply by listening to them, suggesting, "People solve problems more effectively if they can be logical and analytical. Emotions interfere with objectivity."[15] In these terms, healing can be an equalizing and normalizing practice,

12. World Health Organization, "Burn-out."
13. Klotz and Bolino, "Do You Really Know."
14. Horsman, *Servant-Leaders in Training*, 98.
15. Burley-Allen, *Listening*, 113.

especially if some wrong needs to be made right. And when I say "practice," I mean it requires active participation.

- Organizationists Liz Fosslien and Mollie West Duffy have a simple, direct approach to healing that is steeped in humility: admit the mistake, say you're sorry, and clarify how next time will be different.[16] Here's how that interaction might play out with a donor: "You requested a tax letter for your accountant, and we provided the wrong details. I'm very sorry about that. We've made some updates to your details in our database so this information will be correct in the future."

If the situation isn't so fiery, sometimes it helps to think about who our donors are—as professionals and people— and where they may be in their work or home lifecycles. For example, if a donor is an accountant, their schedule may be hectic and stressful during tax season (typically the month of April in the US) each year. For the parents of a newborn, their lives are likely busier and less predictable than normal. In instances like those, keep your outreach and engagement light and low stress. Perhaps consider sending notes to wish them well, rather than trying to schedule a meeting to discuss a renewal of their annual gift or inviting them to an event.

Within the matrix of healing, fundraisers must also look inward. We aren't always as kind with ourselves as we are with our supporters. I have believed this for much of my career, and even more so since spring 2020. We all know colleagues who give (or *serve*) so much that it begins to take a major toll. After enough time it can prevent them from doing not only the work they need to do but from taking care of themselves.

Too much of an unchecked, *servant-first* disposition may result in servant-leaders becoming organizational martyrs. Leadership coach Songya Kesler suggests, "In this state, we believe that our own well-being comes second to the team's or organization's success and we *proudly* suffer to keep the team and organization

---

16. Fosslien and West Duffy, *No Hard Feelings*, 142–143.

afloat."[17] That is not servant-leadership, it is service to a fault. You'll read about one such experience in this section's story from Becky Endicott. As you read Becky's story, think about whether it reminds you of any personal experience when your wick finally burned too short. Like a frog in slowly boiling water, we don't always realize we're burnt out or broken down until it's too late.

To *heal* from this type of experience, it is imperative that fundraisers take necessary breaks. Remote and hybrid work have made it particularly difficult for many nonprofiteers to take time away. Our workdays now have fewer and fewer boundaries; we begin earlier and end later. While writing this book, I was surprised to learn that nearly a dozen non-academic colleagues were taking sabbaticals. Most by choice, but some by strong request from their organizations. As workers, in many ways I believe we have brought this on ourselves. More than half of us (American workers especially) don't use our available vacation time, resulting in more than $65 billion in lost benefits we earned![18]

- When you need it—and especially before you think you need it—mark downtime on your calendar to ensure you are truly offline. Psychologist Art Markman said, "The organization is not going to fall apart if you go away. And frankly, if the organization does fall apart because you went away, there's a bigger problem than 'you' in that situation."[19] You don't need to go far or even go anywhere, for that matter. In *Joy from Fear*, psychologist Carla Marie Manly said, "The simple act of imagining a future positive event can induce a sense of joy and well-being."

  Formally work those breaks into your annual or ongoing work plans to help stave off invariably unintended periods of stress. And as part of that planning, make sure colleagues are baseline cross-trained to support some of your core tasks while you're out. (I realize this is more difficult for some functional

17. Kesler, "Servant Leadership Shadows."
18. McCarthy, "Americans Wasted."
19. Beard, "Interview with Art Markman."

areas than others.) Otherwise you risk returning to a situation where you're once again buried under the work you left.

> **STORY: Forging Forward after Breaking Down**
> Becky Endicott, a twenty-year health-care fundraising leader in Oklahoma, told me about a time when she knew that "something wasn't right." It started small—brain fog, detachment, feeling like forty cups of espresso were coursing through her body at night, and difficulty finding joy. The final straw came as a full-blown panic attack while studying for the CFRE exam—racing heart, uncontrollable tears, and an acute sense of fear. The watershed moment resulted in therapy, medication, breathing exercises, and most importantly, rest. *Healing* for Becky meant taking ninety days of FMLA (Family and Medical Leave Act) for a break, followed by reimagining a balanced career path. The result? A resignation from one job to co-found We Are For Good (mentioned earlier), the new media company devoted to elevating and democratizing fundraising, where she rediscovered her joy for this work. Becky learned that as a fundraiser, you must hold space for the power of your own voice, your own choices, your own boundaries, and your own self-care. This can look different for everyone, but she makes it seem seamless with these suggestions: "Find community, give yourself quiet, offer remote work, encourage staff to attend important family events that occur during the workday, practice internal rituals, check in on your people often, and gently follow-up when the answer to *how are you?* is met with *fine*."

Although critical to the work of social impact, fewer than one percent of the 12.5 million US nonprofit workforce are fundraisers.[20][21] When the Covid-19 pandemic first struck, it was conservatively estimated that more than 1.6 million nonprofiteers' jobs vanished. Many returned, but by the end of 2021, more than

20. Bureau of Labor Statistics, "Occupational Outlook: Fundraisers."
21. Salamon and Newhouse, "The 2020 Nonprofit Employment."

one-quarter remained lost.[22] Clearly, the nonprofit sector is not immune from what has been called "the great reshuffling" or "the great resignation." As these lost jobs slowly continue to return, and as nonprofits seek to hire and onboard new fundraisers, looking inward as part of healing is imperative. The simple act of providing clarity and openness in fundraiser job descriptions is another strong opportunity.

- For organizations and hiring managers, consider being overly transparent and obvious about important details in job postings. Many fundraising position descriptions are carbon copies of one another that focus heavily on subjective, unspecific details—e.g., "Must be able to communicate effectively" or "Model behavior that will help cultivate a culture of philanthropy." These notes are important, and we shouldn't abandon them entirely. However, descriptions that focus on fundraising targets, the size of the donor portfolio, realistic expectations within the first year, and salary details go a long way in equitably recruiting the best talent to participate healthily in an organization's philanthropic efforts.

Let's circle back about that. . .

- Try to do the right thing by your donors. Make up for organizational mistakes and give them space and time when they might need space and time.

- Healing others means healing inside first, which begins with taking space and breaks ourselves.

- Healing starts at the beginning by recruiting fundraisers clearly and honestly.

PERSUASION

As we nonprofiteers seek to raise money, we often use stories. We lean into storytelling to inspire donors and encourage (persuade)

22. Newhouse, "Covid-19 Jobs."

them to be involved with our work. And why wouldn't we? Stories are a way to translate not only our organizational values but the values of the people we serve, and nonprofits have amazing examples. In doing all this, we ask people to part with their hard-earned financial resources that allow our organizations to do big, great things.

However, storytelling can be something of a Trojan horse, enveloping unpleasant or unkind details in a shroud of positivity. Most organizations don't do this intentionally, but they sometimes fail to notice sinister or backhanded issues when stories push false feelings of understanding or sympathy. In telling the stories of the people and communities we serve, and attempting to lift up those protagonists, we should ensure we are not telling the wrong stories. Moreover, we must not demoralize people or their communities.

Nonprofit consultant Rachel D'Souza Siebert calls this exploitative practice *poverty porn*, which calls out someone's condition "to generate the necessary sympathy for gaining supporters to a given cause."[23] Language or content that focuses on the individuals and institutions we intend to "improve" or "save" can paint an unintentionally negative picture. We don't need to look far to see these types of messages, especially in recent years as media outlets have pummeled us with trauma, illness, war, and other catastrophes. What sometimes seems right and effective for our organizations may fail to spotlight someone's personal power and dignity.

- We can improve on this by being collaborative, being honest with how stories will be used, and keeping in touch with those whose stories we tell. Especially with communications collateral like brochures or videos, make sure you not only have the rights to use certain images (you'd be surprised how often this step gets missed) but that they are showing people in a dignified, humane way. Our organizations should not portray our stakeholders at their lowest, worst-possible moments. (Sorry, Sarah McLachlan and those sad animal commercials. . .) And if your organization has the means, financial or otherwise, consider providing some support for the people whose stories

23. Siebert, "Does Your Organization's Storytelling."

you are telling. It would be an incredible demonstration of trust to make those relationships mutually supportive.

> **STORY: Showcasing a Fuller Truth**
> James Roh, a photojournalist in Utah, spoke with me about dignity in storytelling. For a work assignment he was tasked with documenting the resettlement journey of "Isaac," a recent refugee from East Africa who had been in refugee camps long before they met. Some of the photos James captured were taken at the height of Isaac's journey to the US, which brought some anxiety and reflection. Ultimately, though, James believed his goal was to fight misconceptions about refugees. Nonprofits often lean into the challenging aspects of someone's story to raise funds, but many of James's images simply featured Isaac smiling, enjoying his work, and even test driving a new car. "I'm trying to tell a bigger, truthful, and more accurate story about the world," James mused. "Even if sometimes that means my photos won't rack up likes on Instagram."

Another element of persuasion can be found in the simple ways we make requests of donors. You might be familiar with the fundraising maxim, "If you ask for money, you may get advice, and if you ask for advice, you may get money." Rather than trying to manipulate or coerce a donor to support a specific cause or program, take the longer, *persuasive* road and invite a conversation about mutual benefits that rely on their expertise and experience.

- For example, if a donor is passionate about Asian youth in a certain neighborhood, consider framing your inquiry around that enthusiasm: "You have such a long history with the Youth Korean Council in the downtown area. Our program would be great for primary-age students in that neighborhood, though we haven't been successful in making inroads. Would you be open to a conversation and to share guidance on how we might best approach that community?" Depending on the donor's response, consider taking this one step further by exploring not simply *how* the organization might achieve its goal but what would be the best outcome.

Greenleaf believed that one might be persuaded "upon arrival at a feeling of rightness about a belief or action *through one's own intuitive sense*."[24] Asking donors for advice invites their intuition and experience, and in this way, you might be able to expand on your request. "If this new partnership with the Youth Korean Council is successful, how might that look? Do you think it might open more doors for us with the community?"

Finally, if the situation allows, consider persuading a donor in terms of talking about the varying degrees to which their donation will provide impact. It doesn't happen all the time, but I have seen donors' gifts scale up significantly depending on how well I present details about the different possible outcomes of their support. In nature, some animals will grow to a size allowable by their environment. This is a process called indeterminate growth, and I believe some donors' gifts can grow indeterminately in the same way.

- Consider judiciously (and honestly) sharing details about gift ranges. Some fundraisers believe ranges limit the amount a donor will give. However, done carefully, it might persuade a donor to think bigger than they otherwise would. I once spoke with a supporter about honoring his late wife's legacy. She believed deeply in the power of education, and compared to their capacity, they were making meaningful (but smaller) gifts each year of $5,000. The husband told me plainly, "I want her memory to live on in the work of this organization she loved so much." In response, I shared a few options, suggesting, "Your annual gift of $5,000 will allow us to teach twenty-five students this year, as it has for many years. We will teach 250 students this year with $50,000. And if you're open to the idea of us teaching 125 students *every* year, we can achieve that with an endowment gift of $500,000. What will be the most meaningful impact for you?"

24. Greenleaf, *The Power of Servant Leadership*, 85.

Let's circle back about that...

- Persuade philanthropy by showcasing people in their most dignified light. While *poverty porn* might raise some short-term dollars, it does not serve the greater good.

- Donors may be persuaded if, instead of money, we invite their advice and guidance on opportunities for our organizations.

- Philanthropy may scale up if we can demonstrate greater impact through greater giving.

AWARENESS

Awareness may be the most easily digestible servant-leader behavior. In his seminal essay, *The Servant as Leader*, Greenleaf suggested, "A qualification for leadership is that one can tolerate a sustained wide span of awareness so that one better *sees it as it is*."[25] The way I think about this is with the phrase "read the room."

Many fundraisers have experienced donor meetings where someone—a peer, executive director, board member—made a comment that was unsavory, or flat out incendiary. Or perhaps you've watched one of those same people solicit a donation when the moment was not right.

During the height of the pandemic, I recall a Zoom meeting when, unprompted, one of my peers asked a donor, "Don't you think it's wild how many civil liberties and freedoms we are giving up these days?" It was an odd comment to make during a global health crisis, especially to a donor who was openly politically liberal. They believed in the protective measures being made by local civic leaders, like mask mandates and restaurant capacity limits. What's more, this donor was a long-time volunteer for a progressive political candidate. My colleague purely lacked a certain level of introspection, which is a significant part of practicing awareness. (And at times it truly is a practice.) To no surprise, the conversation ended soon after the comment was made.

25. Greenleaf, *Servant Leadership*, 40.

Greenleaf believed real leaders see things as they are and that they have a unique capacity to point the direction and guide the way. As fundraisers, we know the direction isn't always clear, and to begin this process, it helps to look inward. You must be right with yourself before you can be right with your donors. The best fundraisers I've seen are the ones who understand this keen sense of self-awareness.

- Being self-aware requires fully giving of ourselves to a conversation. But many times we remain tethered to external stimulants: televisions in a crowded room, ringing cellphones, vibrating smartwatches. Some research has found that these devices can distract us for almost thirty seconds.[26] That's *twice* as long as the chorus of Bon Jovi's mega hit, "Livin' On A Prayer." Greenleaf suggested, "Able leaders are usually sharply awake,"[27] and to allow that awake-ness requires untethering ourselves from that which distracts us from being aware.

For at least ten to fifteen minutes before any meeting or conversation, turn away from distractions. Turn off the big screens and leave the medium and small screens in your bag, car, or out of sight. (I know you may think you're the one person on Earth who doesn't get distracted by their technology, but you do.) If you work remotely—or even if you don't—buffer the space between meetings by scheduling them in thirty- or forty-five-minute increments, giving yourself fifteen to thirty minutes to decompress and prepare for what's next.

Once you are focused and *sharply awake*, as Greenleaf urged, try to imagine what will be different—changed, enhanced, or improved—when your fundraising goals have been achieved. In his masterful book, *The Fifth Discipline*, systems thinking authority Peter Senge encourages leaders to imagine that some goal has been achieved or realized. "Then ask yourself this question: If I actually had this, what would it get me?"[28]

26. Lasley, "Two Empty Seats."
27. Greenleaf, *Servant Leadership*, 42.
28. Senge, *The Fifth Discipline*, 208.

Many nonprofits have lofty, unrealistic expectations about fundraising. They may suggest, "We are a $3 million organization, but our budget should be $5 million!" I have been on the receiving end of boards and senior managers pushing for those types of goals. But as the National Council of Nonprofits notes, fewer than ten percent of nonprofits in the US have budgets over $1 million.[29] Further, American nonprofit revenues have historically increased an average of only 3.9 percent per year.[30]

- Consider what exactly would be the benefit(s) of being larger, even if great philanthropic dollars were available. Would those additional resources provide more well-paying jobs? Would the under-served in your community be better served and given access to more basic, human needs? Ask Senge's pivotal question to help keep reality grounded, and to encourage stakeholders to be aware and informed. And push back if you are asked to create revenue budgets that drastically exceed the national 3.9 percent average or your organization's historical fundraising progress. (The following story is a good example of a great caveat.)

STORY: Envisioning a Bold Fundraising Future by Being Aware

Brittany Veneris, director of fundraising at Movember, enlightened me on the organization's plans to ramp up US fundraising. While Movember raises an impressive $100 million-plus around the world each year, less than 20 percent of those revenues come from the US market. Brittany surprised me by sharing their vision to triple those figures by 2025. When I prompted her with the 3.9 percent average revenue growth statistic, she smiled, paused, and proceeded to tell me about Movember's robust strategy to engage corporate partners, bolster programmatic collaborations, and build a major gifts program. And their strong future plans are built on a strong awareness of their current reality. During the darkest days of the pandemic, when

29. National Council of Nonprofits, "Nonprofit Impact."
30. Statista, "Revenues of Reporting Nonprofit Organizations."

organizations' donations were down an average of 31 percent,[31] Movember held the line with a decrease of only 13 percent. This inspired the organization to dream big with their goals. But this growth isn't simply meant to put them in a larger funding bracket. One of Movember's core values is to create *remarkable experiences*, and as Brittany told me, "We can't be in all the places all the time. Our community helps our organization grow and thrive." Committing to transformative revenue growth will allow the organization to do just that.

Back to Greenleaf's idea about leaders who see things as they are, one of the very best ways to cultivate awareness is to get people in your organization's doors. Sometimes this is figurative, though I am talking about volunteerism. Volunteers get to see your work in real time, often experiencing the direct impact your organization has on its stakeholders. But what does this have to do with philanthropy? Almost 40 percent of donors say they would volunteer with an organization before making a gift, and nearly two-thirds of nonprofit donors also say they recently volunteered![32]

- If you have immediate needs or opportunities to volunteer, make those easy for people to discover. Post about them often on social media, feature them in your e-newsletters, and have visible, bold, clickable boxes on your website. Also, make sure your volunteer opportunities are showcased elsewhere like AllForGood, Idealist, and VolunteerMatch. If you need technical support, there are great free and low-cost options like Signup.com and Volgistics, and countless others including Airtable, CERVIS, Duplie, Keela, Symba, and many more.

Before we move on, remember my peer who made the unsavory comment about civil liberties? I spoke with them about why the meeting went south and realized I was part of the issue. It wasn't going to change their personal feelings about mask mandates and lockdowns, but I channeled my inner healer vis-à-vis Liz Fosslien

31. Urban Institute, "Nonprofit Trends."
32. Fidelity Charitable, "The Role of Volunteering."

and Mollie West Duffy. I admitted I should've prepared us better, apologized for dropping that ball, and committed to providing them with more information before any subsequent meetings. We ended up being a great duo on future fundraising visits.

Let's circle back about that...

- Turn off, or away from, devices and other distractions for ten to fifteen minutes before you meet with a donor. And schedule shorter meetings with bigger breaks in between.

- Bigger isn't always better. Be aware by having realistic conversations with leadership about sustainable future fundraising goals.

- The road to becoming a donor sometimes begins with volunteerism. Create those opportunities and make them visible to all.

FORESIGHT

Greenleaf was clearly interested in the future. He may have even been concerned with it. He ruminated on how most people, especially leaders, seldom have all the information they need to make good future decisions, irrespective of their age or experience. In *The Servant as Leader*, he wrote that leaders must have *"a sense for the unknowable* and be able to *foresee the unforeseeable."*[33]

I prefer to think about foresight in this way: it's like hindsight with prescription glasses.

Never was this more prophetic for me than an experience in February 2020. A professor friend asked me to speak with her class about strategic planning. Part of the students' assignment for the semester was to create a plan for a real, local nonprofit. I vividly remember the first question asked by one of the students: "Do you think we should create a five- or ten-year plan?" I chuckled and then spoke with the group about realistic timelines for organizations as they look to the future. And wouldn't you know it? Six weeks after my visit, the entire world began closing its doors in response to the

33. Greenleaf, *Servant Leadership*, 35.

Covid-19 pandemic. (Many nonprofits have strategic plans, but at the time I wasn't aware of any organizations whose plans included a section titled, "How to Survive a Global Health Crisis.")

While writing this book, the world was moving (slowly) beyond the pandemic and toward what appears to be some version of a recession. And both of these experiences came on the heels of years of financial, social, and political uncertainty. What is becoming increasingly clear, especially in fundraising, is that the future is unpredictable. But that doesn't mean we can't plan for it—and it certainly doesn't mean we shouldn't try. With an uncertain future, consider a notion I happily borrow from former professional poker player Annie Duke: reversibility. Duke suggests some bold, reversible moves organizations can make, like using furloughs over layoffs, and salary cuts over furloughs.[34] But there are other ways to be reversible, some of which warrant an awareness of staff strengths. During the pandemic, the Blanton Museum (Austin, Texas) refocused custodial staff around other organizational needs, like helping to research new artists and even writing thank-you notes to donors.[35]

- One of the original definitions of the word *pivot* described a hinge, like the fulcrum under a seesaw that allows it to move back and forth. That word has been used a lot in recent years, but if your organization were struck with a demand to refashion operations quickly and temporarily, how might you pivot as you look forward?

  Do you have unused office space to sublease to a small nonprofit or startup? Can some of your staff offer expertise to other organizations on a fee-for-service basis? If you need to grow your operations, could you pause one less critical area of your programming and briefly redirect those dollars to a part-time or contract fundraiser to ensure revenue keeps flowing? (That one requires some serious, honest, and difficult internal conversations.)

34. Duke, "3 Ways to Prepare."
35. Cascone, "By Redeploying Her Staff."

In nonprofit fundraising, one of the terminal experiences is this age-old notion: "We do it this way because we have always done it this way." Greenleaf wondered about such an issue, curious that if "too many who presume to lead do not see more clearly, and in defense of their inadequacy, they all the more strongly argue that the 'system' must be preserved."[36] Those with enough experience of the past and passion for the future can create positive, *foreseeable* outcomes. They become the tide that raises all boats.

- Foresight sometimes demands admitting there are things we simply don't know. (I'll be the first to admit this is hard to admit!) In raising money for a specific program or initiative, the best fundraisers in the world don't always know as much as the program officers and others who are leading the work.

To be visionary can mean taking a back seat to the experts, especially when that approach is best for the relationship with a donor. In these situations, looking ahead means bringing those who are historically (and organizationally) knowledgeable to the table. Invite them to brainstorming meetings, ask their opinions about which funders make sense for projects, and openly discuss ways to demonstrate the future impact of these initiatives with external stakeholders.

STORY: Looking Ahead with Experts in Tow

This tale is my own. When the Covid-19 pandemic first broke, the organization where I worked was two months away from our annual fundraising event—a 1,600-person luncheon that featured a presentation about important demographic research. Like many organizations at the time, the prevailing attitude was "let's wait and see what happens," but donors began calling to ask about our plans. Knowing how valuable the research was for donors, businesses, civic leaders, and even other nonprofits, I believed the show must go on, somehow. My instinct was for us to offer the program online. (This was months before every nonprofit began hosting a litany of virtual events.) Realizing I had no idea how to pull this off, I wrangled smarter people than

36. Greenleaf, *Servant Leadership*, 28–29.

me—our leadership and board, some of our core sponsors, and a creative production company—and together we dreamed up a plan that was safe and interesting. The result? A virtual program that was watched by more than 4,000 people, higher net revenue than in-person luncheons had ever garnered before, and equally as important, countless donors who were grateful we persevered.

Sometimes, in the important space between hindsight and foresight, something gets lost. When this happens, we aren't always able to focus on a solution. There is a necessary, additional step in the process that demands some patience. We don't often give ourselves or our decisions the opportunity to be still. I have long referred to this skill as the "art of settling." Think of it like music and how powerful the rests (pauses) between notes can be. Sometimes those rests are more important than the notes themselves, like those between the first few notes of AC/DC's "Back In Black:" *dun (rest) dun-dun-dun (rest) dun-dun-dun (rest)*. Or for my Gen Z crowd, the pause between "I'm the bad guy (*long rest*) duh" in Billie Eilish's song, "bad guy." These momentary pauses leave space for reflection and growth, allowing something to settle and be truly useful.

- Consider filling those pauses by being mindful of how you feel while bits of information incubate. For instance, let's say a donor does something to make you angry, sad, or even excited. Liz Fosslien and Mollie West Duffy say those are *irrelevant* emotions that have a relatively short shelf life.[37] In those experiences, you might consider taking a break and brushing those feelings aside. However, if you leave a conversation or meeting feeling *relevant* emotions like anxiety or regret—e.g., you wish you had shared more news about a program or funding opportunity—you may want to ruminate on that feeling. Doing so may get you a bit closer to the all the information you need to make good, forward-looking decisions.

37. Fosslien and West Duffy, *No Hard Feelings*, 84.

Let's circle back about that...

- In uncertain times, or planning for uncertain times, consider approaching the future through a lens of reversibility.

- Having foresight means realizing you're not the smartest person in a room, because sometimes you're not. Make sure those experts are there to help you see the future.

- Think about how you feel about, or after, a donor interaction. Relevant emotions like anxiety or regret are worth minding, while irrelevant emotions like excitement or anger may not be.

CONCEPTUALIZATION

Greenleaf believed conceptualization to be "the prime leadership talent."[38] Methodical fundraisers may be able to solicit targeted gifts from a specific group of donors, but only a truly *conceptual* leader in philanthropy will influence supporters to see the bigger picture. If you agree that leadership is fundamentally about *influence* (from Peter Northouse's earlier definition), then the nature of conceptualization may in fact be the most important thing.

But what *is* the bigger picture? It is not simply the slate of programs or events a nonprofit produces. Sometimes it can be the inner workings of an organization itself, and for this, we can look more into systems thinking. While Peter Senge's work on this is incredibly popular, I also appreciate Virginia Anderson and Lauren Johnson's book, *Systems Thinking Basics*. In it they suggest systems exist as constructs "that leave evidence of their presence," notably the *events, patterns*, and *structures* that comprise the reality of everyday organizational experiences.[39]

I often use the following driving analogy when talking about events, patterns, and structures with unfamiliar audiences. Imagine driving on a busy, three-lane highway in a rush, and you are laser-focused on the car in front of you. It's slowing down, but you can't

---

38. Greenleaf, *Servant Leadership*, 45.
39. Anderson and Johnson, *Systems Thinking Basics*, 5.

tell because the driver isn't stepping on their brakes. That's an *event*. Since you're not looking at the other lanes of traffic, you're missing the *pattern* that all the other cars are braking because there's a big wreck up ahead. Because of this, you fail to see the whole *structure*. When the car in front of you comes to a halt, you smash right into it.

Fundraisers might want an example closer to home. Here's one from my days managing development efforts at a small nonprofit.

A donor had been mailing a physical check to our office every month, and the operations manager was receiving and depositing the checks quickly. (This colleague did not practice the "art of settling" I wrote about earlier.) In their process, they were coding the checks as earned program revenue, not contributed or donated revenue as they should have been. In doing so, the fundraising team was not learning about the donations, nor were the gifts showing up in any reports we pulled from our database. This lack of information prevented us from engaging appropriately with the donor: thanking them, sharing organizational materials, or simply inviting them to conversations about why they continued to support our work.

Have you had something like this happen in your nonprofit? These *events* may seem unique and disconnected, but when you zoom out and notice they are happening, *patterns* begin to emerge. I did not realize this was occurring until the donor called me one afternoon with a question. After talking with the operations manager, I realized I had made certain assumptions about their responsibilities. In doing so, a *structure* of good practice never arose.

To conceptualize the right thing to do for our organizations and our donors requires processes, but it also requires some creative action. This calls for a bit of human effort, which doesn't always happen. Why? Because human beings tend to make things slower and less efficient than many of the automated systems on which we rely. It might seem counterintuitive to add another meeting or another task to an already long list of responsibilities, though to do right by our donors (and our organizations), those are things we really must do.

- In organizations that have been around for many years, test the systems you currently have. Talk with a donor about their recent experience making a gift and examine the process from their perspective. I promise you, if a donor appreciates your organization, they'll appreciate a conversation like this. Did they receive an appropriate response, like a confirmation email, thank-you letter, or tax receipt? How long did it take? Look inside too at when that donor's gift was received. How did the transaction play out between your organization's different departments?

    Separately, try inviting a trusted (and ideally impartial) external person to make a new gift and see how the system works for them. And like a good servant-leader listener, take their feedback seriously. Make sure you try these approaches before any significant giving campaign, like an annual appeal, giving day, or a text-to-give event. Donors want good things for our nonprofits, and although not everything needs streamlining, the fundamental systems should work as smoothly as possible.

Inside our organizations, conceptualizing human effort requires reflecting on the skills and abilities of those who lead and guide fundraising. "Servant-leaders seek to nurture their abilities to dream great dreams," John Burkhardt and Larry Spears wrote.[40] As employees we can think of this as personal mastery, in the way Peter Senge affirmed, "People with high levels of personal mastery are continually expanding their ability to create the results in life they truly seek."[41] And for those of us who manage people responsible for fundraising, we must help conceptualize their paths to success.

- A fundraiser may seek to become a certified fund raising executive (CFRE), participate in low- or no-cost workshops with their local Association of Fundraising Professionals or United Way chapters, take online courses with Candid.org or the Lilly Family School of Philanthropy, or listen to *hundreds* of free podcasts available.

---

40. Burkhardt and Spears, *Servant-Leadership*, 4.
41. Senge, *The Fifth Discipline*, 178.

If you manage fundraisers or fundraising staff, consider guiding values-based conversations with them individually and as a group. I have seen philanthropy teams' productivity skyrocket by assessing individuals' strengths and collective values and figuring out how those elements coexist. This can be as simple or involved as you wish, like having everyone take a DiSC, Clifton Strengths (formerly *StrengthsFinder*), VIA Character Strengths Survey, or Enneagram assessment, and then discussing the results. (One of my favorite exercises comes from Jim Kouzes and Barry Posner's *The Leadership Challenge Workbook* in Chapter Four. It clarifies individual values and demonstrates how to put them into action across teams and organizations.)

If possible, based on what you learn from these assessments, put some financial resources aside to bring in a coach or consultant to team build.

Beyond building skills, there is an element to conceptualization that warrants, as visionary leadership expert Dr. Mary McFarland suggested, "taking some time to truly see if there is an understanding of what we're talking about."[42] This in some ways mimics the characteristics of *awareness*. In a global sense—literally in working across cultures or engaging with philanthropists who may be dissimilar from ourselves—McFarland advises further, "In the broader context of servant-leadership, if we truly want to be wiser ourselves as well, what do we pay attention to? Are we willing to ask questions to be sure that our concept or our conceptualization is similar?"

- As the world around us grows simultaneously smaller and more nuanced, we increasingly engage with individuals from different backgrounds. Heeding McFarland's advice, this can be as simple as making sure you are comfortable with the way someone spells or pronounces their name. You can say, very simply, "You have such a lovely name, and I notice from our emails there is a diacritical accent above the ó—how do

---

42. Ferch et al., *Conversations*, 168.

I correctly pronounce it?" And if a donor introduces themselves with a unique name you might have trouble with, make sure you repeat it back and work it into the conversation a few times. People really do love the sound of their own names, so we better get them right! The same is true with other personal details, like preferred pronouns.

> **STORY: Pick up Your Head to See the Full Picture**
> In Massachusetts, nonprofit strategist and consultant Julia Campbell was working with an addiction treatment and suicide prevention agency when she began to notice an older patron bringing in $10 cash donations every Friday. He would give the $10 bills to the receptionist and never ask for a receipt or recognition. Wanting to be *wiser herself*, as McFarland advised, Julia spoke with the patron. What did she learn? Ten dollars was the weekly allowance the patron used to give his son who had passed away, and he believed the nonprofit's mission might have helped keep his son alive. "If you simply talk with people, if you just pick up your head," Julia shared with me, "you'll realize the power of giving felt by those who support your causes." Because Julia helped the organization *conceptualize* who this patron was, he became more involved and even joined their board.

Let's circle back about that...

- Test your organization's structures by examining the start-to-finish process of a recent gift or a brand new one.

- Apt colleagues have the best chance at conceptualization. Make sure your people have the training and skills they need through certifications, courses, or workshops.

- Conceptualizing is simply understanding, and we should take some time to understand the basics about our donors, like how they pronounce their own names or preferred pronouns.

STEWARDSHIP

There is no shortage of definitions for the word "stewardship." They range in context from religion to nature to resources and beyond. However, irrespective of the context, at the heart of the word is *trust*. Inside organizations, Greenleaf suggested many different people play "significant roles in holding their institutions in trust for the greater good of society"[43]—from board members to staff to CEOs and beyond.

In nonprofits, we routinely think of stewardship in terms of how we share our appreciation for donations and grants. Those actions include how quickly we get thank-you letters in the mail or the paper stock on which those letters are printed. No fundraiser in their right mind would suggest being appreciative *isn't* valuable, but expressing our gratitude is only a small part of stewardship. We must also demonstrate how we are using donor funds appropriately to lead impact through our work. This is important for many reasons. Of course, the Internal Revenue Service necessitates that we send documentation for donations over $250.[44] However, a statutory requirement is where a process should begin, not where it ends. We are at a pivotal moment when it comes to encouraging and ensuring trust with donors, as fewer than one in five donors report having high levels of trust in nonprofits.[45]

Here's something many organizations fail to admit or realize: stewardship does not need to be flashy, burdensome, or overly complicated. Yet if nonprofits wish to keep their supporters happy, informed, and engaged, stewarding honestly and regularly is so important.

It is estimated that nonprofit organizations retain roughly 45 percent of their donors from year to year, and almost the same number of donors (44 percent) suggest the reason they stop giving is because of poor or lacking communication.[46] It does not matter how big or small the organization is, stewardship must be part of its ongoing work. In fact, the National Council of Nonprofits estimates

43. Greenleaf, *The Power of Servant Leadership*, 7.
44. Internal Revenue Service, "Charitable Contributions."
45. Give.org, "Give.org Donor Trust Report 2022."
46. Bloomerang, "A Guide to Donor Retention."

that most nonprofits (75 percent) have annual budgets under $100,000.[47] Even though smaller shops may lack the infrastructure of their larger peers, the same responsibility remains.

- Begin by assessing what is possible given your organizational resources of staff, budget, and time. A basic stewardship matrix is a useful tool. Such a document will help organizations outline opportunities for the basics of keeping in touch with supporters, like recognition on a website or in social media, when and how to share news about impact, receipt of holiday/New Year's cards, and other ways. It can also delineate who donors hear from throughout their journey—development staff, CEO, board members—and when. A simple, editable, downloadable version with examples can be found online at TheNonprofiteers.com.

Once an organization figures out the mechanics of its stewardship—like who communicates with whom, when, and how—it must consider the types of messages it produces and shares with supporters. Of course, this includes the basic methods of thanking and appreciating donors, and it can also feature novel ways of making them comfortable and familiar with an organization's people.

- In early written communication with donors, like thank-you emails and letters, consider featuring a "statement of commitments." This statement can be simple, spotlighting some of the inflexible guarantees your organization will make to a donor. Such commitments might be that a donor will always know who to contact if and when they have a question, instead of a generic "info@nonprofit.org" email address. Or that they will always know how donated funds are being used, even if those funds are for general operating support. One thing I've also done in many organizations is include brief biographies (two or three sentences) of key staff with whom donors might interact. This little act can go a long way in painting a human picture of an organization, especially in an industry where the average tenure of fundraising staff is under two years.[48]

47. National Council of Nonprofits, "Nonprofit Impact."
48. Lively and Vinukonda, "Calculating the Cost."

> **STORY: Building Trust through Hard Truths**
>
> Anne Murphy, an Oregonian fundraiser, shared a story of trust from her time as a university development officer. Before Anne's time, a donor, "Joyce," had created a scholarship fund that went years without being fulfilled. The staff couldn't identify students to receive the funding, nor were they honest with Joyce about the challenges. This frustrated Joyce, eroded trust, and risked a subsequent $2 million estate gift. When a new dean arrived, he proposed a radical idea: tell the truth. Like Fosslien and West Duffy's healing suggestion, he admitted the error, apologized for the good intentions but bad outcomes, and offered to meet with Joyce and discuss a new plan. It was a chilly conversation, but Joyce welcomed a discussion about next steps. Over a three-hour meeting, Joyce enlightened the dean about the impact a similar scholarship had on her—she simply wanted that for others. While she was upset the original gift wasn't meeting its purpose, she was more hurt by the sheer absence of communication. Following the visit, Joyce agreed to a rewrite of the original gift agreement, and even gave the university permission to continue a dialogue about her estate gift. In this way, the dean played a tremendous role in maintaining trust by rebuilding it.

At the end of the day, nonprofits do need to create and share *some* materials with donors. I'm an old soul, and I personally enjoy print and mail pieces. Many organizations create flashy, attractive, and expensive documents like annual reports for donors and other constituents. These items can be costly, but they don't need to be! They can also be rather obscure and feature quirky, unconfirmable figures, like "10,000 community members reached" or "50,000 website visits." Contrarily, Marisa DeSalles and Michelle Flores Vryn inquired, "What do annual reports communicate about us. . . What if we wrote them honestly, for and with the community instead?"[49]

- Consider sharing a simple *impact* report that demonstrates the differences being made by your organization. Several I've done have been small, fold-over postcards that include

49. DeSalles and Vryn, "The Annual Report"

narrative or stories about how a single family, community, or other stakeholder was transformed because of the work. And in talking about impact, you can help donors see how their gifts are making a real difference.

One such impact postcard we created at a former organization had this simple title on the front: "How You Helped Build a Better City," and the narrative explained how donors' critical dollars were spent in service of that *building*. When communicating about impact, be mindful of the language you use. Go beyond the phrase "thanks for your gift" and talk about what is changed, different, or improved because of someone's philanthropy. An example of some differences can be found at the end of the book on pages 71–72.

Let's circle back about that. . .

- Use a stewardship matrix to outline the various ways your small or large organization will steward donors.

- Provide a "statement of commitments" to your donors to let them know their gifts are in good hands, and share some details about your organization's staff.

- Build trust by talking about your organization's impact (outcomes) rather than sending random numbers (outputs) into the void.

COMMITMENT TO THE GROWTH OF PEOPLE

Remember the survey I shared with nonprofit peers? In their own words, most responders suggested servant-leadership is about "putting others first." Doesn't that sound like this characteristic of servant-leadership: growing other people?

Growing other people can sometimes be an aspirational goal, and a difficult one at that. It's difficult to grow programs and budgets, and it's equally difficult to grow the people who lead programs and budgets. Anyone with a modicum of nonprofit experience knows this to be at least partially true. Greenleaf asked questions about growth that get to the heart of what it means to be a servant-leader. And his inquiries were so important, one of them appears one the first page of every volume of the academic publication, *The International Journal of Servant-Leadership*,

> Do those served grow as persons? Do they, *while being served*, become healthier, wiser, freer, more autonomous, more likely themselves to become servants? *And*, what is the effect on the least privileged in society? Will they benefit or at least not be further deprived?

In the orbit of our social impact organizations, "those served" can hold uniquely different meanings. There are the communities nonprofits intend to serve through their missions: children, the disabled, artists, people of color, and so many others. Then there are internal constituents like staff, board members, and other volunteers. Finally, and no less important, are the funders whose trust and resources make much of this work possible. In that order, what follows are suggestions on how you and your organization might *grow* those served.

- First, take a look at communities served by your work. Committing to their growth should involve inviting them to the table. Equity advocate Tamika Butler suggests asking two questions when this situation arises: "Who is this going to impact most, and were they part of the decision-making process? And if those two answers aren't aligned, then you know you have a power imbalance."[50]

  The next time an idea for a project or event is floated, ask Butler's questions. And more than simply asking the questions, make sure you act on the outcome that is discussed by those you invite to the conversation. This is an especially helpful caveat for ideas proposed by staff and volunteers. Their suggestions are no less valid or valuable, however, inviting the view of those who will be directly reached encourages an opportunity for real impact.

---

50. Rice University, "Transportation Equity."

Speaking of staff, next let's consider the internal partners who lead and nurture the work. In the film, *In the Heart of the Sea*, the character Owen Chase is first mate aboard the *Essex*, a whaling ship that would later inspire Herman Melville to pen *Moby Dick*. In one scene, Chase is at odds with a decision made by the captain, one that inevitably sends the ship into a disastrous storm. Though he knew better, Chase chose not to intervene, and this taught the captain a valuable lesson.

- This is a radical example, and I would never advocate for an individual to put themselves or their organization in harm's way. However, for those concerned with the growth of internal organizational communities, consider allowing reasonable space for ownership and failure. This may include inviting a board member to join a committee that's slightly outside their area of expertise or allowing a colleague to propose and execute an initiative the organization has not previously attempted—as long as those ideas are in service of the communities you serve through your mission!

Donors who fund our work are the final community, and they are uniquely important to grow. They can also be the most challenging, and philanthropic advisors Dan Siegel and Jenny Yancey mused about why,

> Even if donors feel uncertain and want to learn more about giving, it is not clear where they can find good advice. . . . While donors may recognize the need to learn and grow, they can be skeptical about the motives of the philanthropy support field. Donors can feel preyed upon. General suspicions about organized philanthropy also arise from public scandals, junk mail, unwanted phone calls, and negative messaging.[51]

Would you be surprised to know Siegel and Yancey's research came from the early 2000s? It's amazing how shockingly relevant their words still are decades later. How then can we commit to growing these trusted partners? Although it may seem counterintuitive, this

---

51. Siegel and Yancy, "Philanthropy's Forgotten Resource."

can be as simple as removing ourselves, as fundraisers, from the conversation entirely.

- Fundraisers and other organizational leaders can be intimidating, sometimes even off-putting. I vividly recall lunch with a donor and our organization's CEO when, after introducing myself, the donor said, curiously, "Ah, the fundraising guy is here. What am I on the hook for?"

If we acknowledge that donors may be skeptical about being guided or advised by organizations directly, we can consider stepping out of the way and connecting them with others who have already walked the path. You may have heard this referred to as "peer-to-peer" engagement or fundraising. This might include a one-time prospect who has grown to become a long-time supporter of an organization's programming, or even a board member. These small communities of practice can be intentional, low-stress, peer learning environments that help to build bridges and grow understanding so people share an understanding of perspectives.[52]

STORY: Growing Others by Getting out of the Way
Julie Ordoñez, a Southern California fundraising change agent, spoke with me about stepping out of the way and elevating others to share their story. In her previous role with a regional United Way, Julie invited a volunteer and donor, "Daniel," to tell his story about firsthand experience with homelessness. Having lost his job during the Great Recession in the late 2000s, Daniel was too proud to go back home. He was forced to live in his car, bathe at the YMCA, and apply for jobs using computers at a local library. Nobody would know it by looking at him, but Daniel was exactly the type of person served by the United Way's efforts to curb homelessness and build a stronger community. Their services helped him rebuild his life, and telling his personal story through a lens of dignity was inspiring. What Julie called "powerful vulnerability" was moving and influential—in effect, doubling the number of donors that particular year.

52. National Council of Nonprofits, "Community of Practice."

Let's circle back about that. . .

- Grow your communities by ensuring they have a seat at the table when you dream up programs and initiatives in service of them.

- Allow reasonable space for people to grow by stretching into uncomfortable territory—and perhaps even failing a little bit.

- Ironically, supporting the growth of our donors may not involve us as fundraisers at all. Consider connecting them with other peers (donors) or help to create safe spaces, like communities of practice.

BUILDING COMMUNITY

Merriam-Webster defines community as, "A unified body of individuals." There's a lot to unpack from the brief description, and in organizations more attention is often paid to the *unified body* than to individuals. However, community is a collective, and building a community is nearly impossible without first considering and cultivating its individual members.

Let's revisit Larry Spears's list of ten servant-leader characteristics. Although "building community" may have appeared last, it is no less critical than the other nine. Even the responses from my survey (mentioned earlier) demonstrated that building community is not simply a top quality fundraisers *should* possess, it is *the* top quality respondents believed they bring to the field of philanthropy.

As with many of the servant-leader characteristics, it helps to think in terms of who we are talking about—in this case, which communities we intend to build. Whether a community is internal (staff, leadership, and boards) or external (donors and others), nonprofits must continuously evaluate the consistency with which they engage them all. If we do some things some of the time, exceptions become rules. In this way, things slip, even if we don't intend for them to. The adage "do what you say you'll do" comes to mind, and consistency can simply reflect a cadence of communication.

- Internally, consider building a regular arc of communication about donations. And much like stewardship, these communications do not need to be fancy or overly complicated. They can take the form of a simple donation log you email to staff and leadership when donations arrive in whatever cadence is appropriate—daily, weekly, or something else. These logs should feature basic details like donor names, donation type (gift, grant, stock transfer), designation (general operations, an event, specific program), and whatever else feels appropriate.

The benefit of sharing these details consistently is that internal stakeholders become more familiar with who is supporting an organization. This is especially important for CEOs and other top managers. Fundraising expert Lilya Wagner suggests, "The best and most successful fundraising programs involve the CEO. . . . Unfortunately, too many fundraisers find that CEO involvement, much less leadership, in fundraising efforts is a vain hope."[53] Although revenue generation *can* be left solely to a fundraising team, it does an organization no favors to keep executives and other top managers away from the conversation.

> **STORY: Building Community by Casting a Wide Communication Net**
> I was encouraged to try the recurring donation records from Elliott, an inspiring philanthropy leader I met years ago. What he called a "daily gift log" was the result of feeling like internal communications were dangerously siloed in one of his former organizations, and management was not giving the right attention to philanthropy. "Fundraising was simply not relevant to the rest of the organization," he shared with me. "The gift log was a way to make contributed revenue part of the organization's everyday life." The result of this realization was sending a recurring, end-of-day email to all the fundraisers and the organization's leadership. Over time, the CEO, who was typically absent from discussions around philanthropy, began asking

---

53. Wagner, "Fundraising, the CEO, and Servant Leadership."

questions about various donors and taking an interest in learning about them. With email and phone details included with the log, the CEO even began to ask if it was appropriate to contact donors and share appreciation for their support. That's a huge win for any organization!

Expanding outward by one degree, a community may also feature other nonprofits working in a similar programming space. Some of these organizations may offer services and programs that are similar or even duplicative. These organizations may not even realize it, resulting in what capacity-building leader Tracy Ebarb refers to as "competitive blinders."[54] If organizations fail to address this internally with their staff and boards, they are not likely to address it with funders. John Henry Horsman offers the advice that servant-leaders "encourage others to become involved in projects that challenge them to support and participate in the good of the collective."[55]

- To build this community and *encourage involvement*, as Horsman suggests, consider gathering organizations whose missions or programs align to explore collaborative opportunities, or at the very least, to brand collective or similar efforts. Even further, invite various funders to a conversation about how this *community* of organizations can be strong partners and recipients of their philanthropy.

   In Houston, Texas, six organizations in the college-preparedness space—Breakthrough Houston, BridgeYear, DiscoverU, EMERGE Fellowship, OneGoal, and Posse Foundation—created a "Post-Secondary Success Collaborative" to address overlapping services and how to communicate effectively with a network of funders.[56] (Bonus: One of the ideas I always want to suggest is for organizations with similar missions to cohost fundraising events. Imagine those six organizations above—or any community of nonprofits—producing one luncheon or gala, where they split the revenues *and* expenses!)

54. Ebarb, "Nonprofits Fail."
55. Horsman, *Servant-Leaders in Training*, 99.
56. EMERGE, "Post-Secondary Success Collaborative."

Finally, we can build community with donors by borrowing from a human resources practice called stay interviews. Different from exit interviews, these conversations are designed to explore the reasons why some employees stay at a company while others leave. These exchanges are excellent for improving staff morale and organizational effectiveness, and they are equally useful for those who manage relationships with donors.

- These questions can begin in very simple terms by asking supporters, "Why do you support our organization?" and, "What do you like most about engaging with our organization?" Probing somewhat deeper, you might inquire, "What do you suggest we enhance at our organization?" or, "What might make the time you spend with our organization more meaningful?" or, "Who do you see as our biggest competitor and/or potential collaborator/partner?" Finally, regarding donor recognition, ask simply, "How do you prefer to be recognized?" A mindset of *staying* will encourage funders to stick with an organization. A more thoughtful dive into these six questions can be found at the end of the field guide on pages 73–75.

Let's circle back about that. . .

- Sharing details about gifts, grants, and other support regularly with managers and leaders goes a long way in building internal community.

- Bring together communities of similar organizations and funders to share learning and encourage collective growth.

- To build a community, that community needs to stick around. Ask "stay interview" questions to encourage them to stay and continue being involved.

On Servant-Leadership and Diversity

IN READING THIS BOOK you may have felt, as I felt writing it, a sense of wholesomeness about servant-leadership. In so many ways it is a "feel-good" philosophy. Yet during my research collecting stories and data, it was difficult to find content on diversity as it relates to servant-leadership. This wasn't overly surprising; however, it is a disservice to the social impact sector to keep servant-leadership conversations colorblind.

As I began writing this field guide, I kept trying (and failing) to weave morsels of this topic into the many recommendations. I kept missing the mark and felt a strong urge to pull the conversation out and call attention to it directly.

I felt particularly compelled to expand upon the topic of fundraiser diversity, or lack thereof, because I have a tremendous passion for nonprofit teams and fundraising talent. While a growing body of work is finally beginning to address the diversity of funders and philanthropists more formally (like the great minds in the Community-Centric Fundraising movement), my experience is more closely tethered to growing staff. During the twenty years of my career, I've interviewed hundreds of people for hundreds of roles. Many of them were, and are, fundraisers, so that's where I have something to add to this conversation.

Let me be blunt: the field of fundraising is fairly. . . monochromatic. Our industry's leading trade organization, Association of Fundraising Professionals, touts roughly 30,000 members, of which people of color—those who identify as Black, Hispanic, Native American, Alaskan Native, Pacific Islander, and mixed-race—total fewer than 10 percent.[1] It's a disappointing figure, but it's not surprising.

Beyond simply acknowledging that a more diverse workforce is the right thing, the data back it up. For- and not-for-profit organizations in the top quartile of ethnically diverse staff financially outperform their industry peers by 35 percent. This extends beyond race, as financial returns for organizations with top-quartile diversity in gender outperformed industry peers by 15 percent.[2] Further, organizations with diverse leadership report innovation revenue that is 19 percent higher than their peers.[3]

But in nonprofits, there is a disconnect. The Building Movement Project's 2019 report, *Nonprofit Executives and the Racial Leadership Gap*, suggests nonprofit leaders of color lack access to funding from donors compared to white counterparts. Leaders of color had 14 percent more difficulty accessing individual donors than white peers; 10 percent found it more difficult to access foundation funders.[4]

As with so many areas of social impact, there's a place at the table for improving diversity through, and with, servant-leadership. Customer service leader Kaylene Eckels urges, "Servant leadership is paramount in building a diverse team capable of delivering unprecedented results."[5] As you've read, those results undoubtably increase revenue.

In the spirit of this field guide, here are three ways to boost philanthropy by diversifying fundraising staff utilizing the servant-leader characteristics of *awareness, building community,* and *listening.*

1. Burton, "The Issue of Racism."
2. Hunt, Layton, and Prince, "Diversity Matters."
3. Lorenzo et al., "How Diverse Leadership Teams."
4. Building Movement Project, "Nonprofit Executives."
5. Eckels, "How Servant Leadership Supports Diversity."

- Hiring fundraisers requires being *aware* of what skills are necessary to do the work. For organizations concerned with inherent biases in hiring, consider "blinding" the recruitment process. By concealing certain details about a candidate, their ability to do the fundraising work will be front and center, rather than their educational background, work experience, and other details that may give "traditional" candidates an unfair advantage. As you collect résumés, CVs, and applications, consider using an app like Applied. It can help anonymize the initial process so hiring managers and teams get useful data that can help predict how candidates will do in a real job. (A Harvard report showed that this practice resulted in an almost four-fold jump in the hiring of female musicians, truly putting their skill above all other details.[6])

- Then, *build community* by looking around the room (or Zoom) at the group of people who will engage the candidate once they've moved beyond the blind-application process. If your hiring committee looks like one particular community— e.g., white men—and they don't look like the candidates you're interviewing, what message will that send? A hiring committee that reflects diversity will bring expansive experiences and thoughts to the process.

   This should *not* be a checklist exercise, and if you're having a difficult time creating a diverse committee, you might want to revisit the first bullet point in this section as you continue building your team forward.

- Finally, encourage good *listening* by having the hiring committee reflect individually before you bring them back together to deliberate on their top choices. The word "silo" can be so negative in business, yet if the committee is allowed the space and time to think back on what they read and received during interviews, you remove some of the possibility for group-think—or that the loudest voices in the room will overpower the conversation.

6. Goldin and Rouse, "Orchestrating Impartiality."

Let's circle back about that. . .

- Create a "blind" hiring process that begins with focusing on an awareness of the skills necessary to do the job.
- Build community by ensuring your hiring committee resembles the diversity of the candidates you are trying to engage.
- Cultivate uninterrupted consideration by encouraging the hiring committee to listen and reflect on their own before bringing recommendations back to the group.

You've Reached the End of the Beginning

PSYCHOLOGIST ABRAHAM MASLOW'S *THE Psychology of Science* was novel for its time (1966). In it, he mused, "I suppose it is tempting, if the only tool you have is a hammer, to treat everything as if it were a nail."[1] Maslow wasn't talking about fundraisers, but I see a connection. I have long watched and worked alongside colleagues who treat fundraising as a one-size-fits-all practice. Every donor is a nail. And they, as fundraisers, in trying to secure or increase funding, act like exacting hammers.

But I believe most of us know this not to be true. We know that our prospects and supporters are interesting, unique, and multi-faceted. They come from different backgrounds and experiences, and they engage with our nonprofits for different reasons. Some have a direct experience being served by the mission (like Daniel from Julie's story on page 53). Others may only know about our work through crowdfunding campaigns, attending events as a guest, or what they learn from friends or the news.

In the early 1990s, Karen Maru File and Russ Alan Prince posited there are, in their view, seven "faces" of philanthropy—from their book of the same name. File and Prince distilled what they believed were the overall archetypes of donors: *dynast, socialite, altruist, repayer, investor, devout,* and *communitarian.* There are some limitations to this research, for sure. But I've found it supremely

1. Maslow, *The Psychology of Science*, 15.

helpful to understand that what motivates a business owner can be, and often is, vastly different from what motivates someone who has been distinctly impacted by a nonprofit's work.

Practiced with care, I have seen servant-leadership account for the myriad types of donors in the world. And it provides a roadmap to engage donors thoughtfully and meaningfully in a way that boosts everyone involved.

Respondents to my survey suggested servant-leadership is about *putting others first*. Although this is a noble sentiment, it is simple and a bit reductive—a nod to the proverb, "feed a man a fish." The practice is more influential, as John Burkhardt and Larry Spears affirmed powerfully, "Servant-leadership encourages everyone to balance leading and serving. . . . The end result of this moving back-and-forth between leading and following is to enhance our lives as individuals, and to raise the very possibilities of our many institutions."[2]

Servant-leadership offers innumerable opportunities to boost the field of philanthropy. You've read thirty (technically thirty-three) of those opportunities in this field guide. And they don't simply benefit the communities that nonprofits serve; they are great for organizations' overall fiscal health. James Sipe and Don Frick's research on the high financial returns of servant-led organizations—24.2 percent versus 10.8 percent from other top companies—demonstrates serious impact. As they said, "Most organizations that have implemented Servant Leadership *because it was the right thing to do* have enjoyed benefits others can only dream about."[3]

Can you imagine an executive director, CFO, or board volunteer dismissing that sort of growth for a nonprofit? I can't. Yet the practice has still not largely entered the mainstream. Nor has it been widely attributed to various areas of nonprofit life, especially fundraising.

The many recommendations and personal stories in this field guide demonstrate actionable ways to practice servant-leadership within philanthropy. I hope we can agree on that. And if so, I hope

2. Burkhardt and Spears, *Servant-Leadership*, 3.
3. Sipe and Frick, *Seven Pillars*, 4.

you'll play a part in furthering public discourse and engagement around servant-leadership, social impact, and philanthropy. With a tip of the hat to MLK Jr., I hope you will talk about it everywhere you go.[4] To that end, please visit *TheNonprofiteers.com* to learn more, explore additional resources, and share your own story. Because, as Greenleaf himself suggested, "Nothing of substance will happen unless there are people inside these institutions who are able to (and want to) lead them into better performance for the public good."[5]

If nothing else, my biggest wish is that *The Nonprofiteer's Fundraising Field Guide* opened your eyes to a different way of thinking. Not only to increase revenues but to boost the whole of philanthropy—from staff to communities to the donors who support our efforts.

This isn't easy work. It never has been. But there's a reason more than 100,000 of us wake up every day to do it.

Thank you again, nonprofiteers, and good luck out there!

---

4. King Jr., "Where Do We Go From Here?"

5. Greenleaf, *Servant Leadership*, 16.

The Long and Short of It

The Nonprofiteer's Fundraising Field Guide was purposefully designed and written to be brief and digestible—like you were thumbing through a handful of succinct, useful blog posts. But who can remember dozens of practical recommendations all at once? Here's a summary of the major recommendations to help you boost fundraising through servant-leadership.

LISTENING

- Avoid steamrolling your conversational counterparts, and try to make sure you allow them more space to speak than you.

- Allow that space by leaning into silence. Four or five seconds of quiet can be transformational.

- Create multiple opportunities to listen to your donors by wrapping in technology.

EMPATHY

- Look forward with fresh eyes by not assuming people in your future will behave like everyone from your past.

- Our colleagues sometimes know better than us. Bring them along to help share the full story.

- Free your mind and open your body language to welcome people into your conversation.

HEALING

- Try to do the right thing by your donors. Make up for organizational mistakes and give them space and time when they might need space and time.

- Healing others means healing inside first, which begins with taking space and breaks ourselves.

- Healing starts at the beginning by recruiting fundraisers clearly and honestly.

PERSUASION

- Persuade philanthropy by showing people in the most dignified light. While *poverty porn* might raise some dollars, it does not serve the greater good.

- Donors may be persuaded if, instead of money, we invite their advice and guidance on opportunities for our organizations.

- Philanthropy may scale up if we can demonstrate greater impact through greater giving.

AWARENESS

- Turn off, or away from, devices and other distractions for ten to fifteen minutes before you meet with a donor. And schedule shorter meetings with bigger breaks in between.

- Bigger isn't always better. Be aware by having realistic conversations with leadership about sustainable future fundraising goals.

- The road to becoming a donor sometimes begins with volunteerism. Create those opportunities, and make them visible to all.

FORESIGHT

- In uncertain times, or planning for uncertain times, consider approaching the future through a lens of reversibility.

- Having foresight means realizing you're not the smartest person in a room, because sometimes you're not. Make sure those experts are there to help you see the future.

- Think about how you feel about, or after, a donor interaction. Relevant emotions like anxiety or regret are worth minding, while irrelevant emotions like excitement or anger may not be.

CONCEPTUALIZATION

- Test your organization's structures by examining the start-to-finish process of a recent gift or a brand new one.

- Apt colleagues have the best chance at conceptualization. Make sure your people have the training and skills they need through certifications, courses, or workshops.

- Conceptualizing is simply understanding, and we should take some time to understand the basics about our donors, like how they pronounce their own names or preferred pronouns.

STEWARDSHIP

- Use a stewardship matrix to outline the various ways your small or large organization will steward donors.

- Provide a "statement of commitments" to your donors to let them know their gifts are in good hands, and share some details about your organization's staff.

- Build trust by talking about your organization's impact (outcomes) rather than sending random numbers (outputs) into the void.

COMMITMENT TO THE GROWTH OF PEOPLE

- Grow your communities by ensuring they have a seat at the table when you dream up programs and initiatives in service of them.

- Allow reasonable space for people to grow by stretching into uncomfortable territory—and perhaps even failing a little bit.

- Ironically, supporting the growth of our donors may not involve us as fundraisers at all. Consider connecting them with other peers (donors) or help to create safe spaces, like communities of practice.

BUILDING COMMUNITY

- Sharing details about gifts, grants, and other support regularly with managers and leaders goes a long way in building internal community.

- Bring together communities of similar organizations and funders to share learning and encourage collective growth.

- To build a community, that community needs to stick around. Ask "stay interview" questions to encourage them to stay and continue being involved.

ON DIVERSITY

- Create a "blind" hiring process that begins with focusing on an awareness of the skills necessary to do the job.

- Build community by ensuring your hiring committee resembles the diversity of the candidates you are trying to engage.

- Cultivate uninterrupted consideration by encouraging the hiring committee to listen and reflect on their own before bringing recommendations back to the group.

All My Immeasurable Gratitude

IT TAKES A LOT to write a book. *A lot.* A lot of time, frustration, patience, and people. And like a building or any physical space, the object you see is simply the end product. Before the foundation is poured or a single brick is placed, there is an idea. There are plans. There are conversations and feedback and hundreds—if not thousands—of cups of coffee.

This book is like that.

There is no short list of people who've helped make this field guide you're holding possible. They are my architects, contractors, designers, and end users. I want to share my appreciation with as many of them, here, as I can.

First, my schnitzelween, Huda. You've helped me find the great deal of courage (madness?) necessary to embark on this journey. I've filled our conversations with rants about philanthropy and leadership, and through it you've been mighty patient. You've also let me fill our kitchen table, bookcase, and entire home with countless journals, articles, books, and other things that take up space. It's safe to say, without you, this field guide would have stayed locked away in my mind. Thanks for always being my most perfect key.

To Mom, Dad, Scott, Stacy, and the rest of my "home" family. Thank you for *always* cultivating a tenacious attitude toward learning, growth, and being a staunch enneagram eight. Evan in his forties is only possible because you pushed young Evan to be audacious. (I know that's not always fun to deal with!) And to my

Texas family—the Alsheikhs, Chraibisheikhs, and Tamjidisheikhs—
I adore you beyond words.

To John Bradshaw. Your direction and steadiness keep me
focused, determined, and—although it's not always possible—
humble. In matters of work and friendship we are indeed a
"Dynamic Duo." I hope that will be true for years to come.

To Larry Spears. You opened my eyes to the wonders of
servant-leadership. You encouraged me to dive deeper by asking,
"What do I do now?" Your insights and support guided me to explore servant-leadership within philanthropy. That journey inspired
the words that became *The Nonprofiteer's Fundraising Field Guide*.

To Becky Endicott, Jon McCoy, Julie Confer, and Abby Fox. If
this book were indeed a building, you all would be the art on the
walls. What you're doing with and through We Are For Good is like
Mister Rogers' Neighborhood for social impact. Thank you for giving
this field guide its soul. (Everyone join their FREE community at
WeAreForGoodCommunity.com)

Now, last but in no way least, to the great many others. You
have literally (and I use that word on purpose) made it possible to
build this project. You've offered editorial prowess, commentary,
advice, input, and guidance. Thank you, Tony Albrecht, Bronwyn
Beauchamp, Chris Bertaut, Aubrey Burghardt, Kit Campoy, Marc
Courtade, Ting-Ting Chen, Melinda English, Callie and Joe Gallo,
Jordan Gross, Max Klein, Maria Latta, Rachel Le, Marcie Lou,
Velma Man, Jack McBride, Lauren Postler, Emily Stein, Jayla Sun,
Joe Synan, Michelle Flores Vryn, Quang Vu, Amy Weiss, and Sarah
White.

Appendix One

Donation Acknowledgement Communication Hierarchy

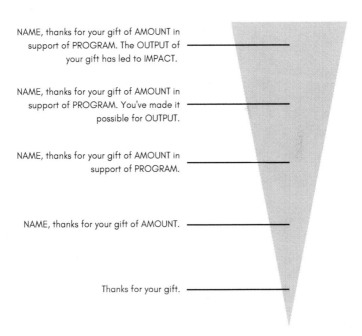

NAME, thanks for your gift of AMOUNT in support of PROGRAM. The OUTPUT of your gift has led to IMPACT.

NAME, thanks for your gift of AMOUNT in support of PROGRAM. You've made it possible for OUTPUT.

NAME, thanks for your gift of AMOUNT in support of PROGRAM.

NAME, thanks for your gift of AMOUNT.

Thanks for your gift.

Here are examples of how each note above can look in practice:

- Evan, thanks for your gift of $50 in support of Joy for Reading. You've helped us reach 100 students this year, and by doing so, we have inspired a love for literature in these young learners.

- Evan, thanks for your gift of $50 in support of Joy for Reading. You've made it possible for us to reach 100 students this year.

- Evan, thanks for your gift of $50 in support of Joy for Reading.

- Evan, thanks for your gift of $50.

- Thanks for your gift.

Appendix Two

Fundraising Stay Interview Questions

THE "BUILDING COMMUNITY" SECTION identified six questions to engage with donors more deeply. I have used each of these questions for many years while cultivating, engaging, and building relationships with individual and institutional supporters. The narrative that follows expands on each of those questions with details on how they might be useful for your work in raising funds and inspiring donors to feel great about supporting your nonprofit.

Why do you support our organization? This is an important question to ask early in the relationship—and equally important to continue asking. If it helps, think of your conversations with donors and potential donors as a developing relationship (friendly, romantic) in which the spark from your first few interactions/dates may be different (and better!) months or years down the road. People—and donors—change, as do their interests. Over time, their wealth and propensity to support may also deepen.

What do you like most about engaging with our organization? It's a positive frame, non-guiding, and I'm often surprised by what the answers reveal. One year, I learned that several donors loved calling the organization and interacting with our receptionist because he was so wonderfully helpful and kind. We knew this as a staff, but we had no idea of his impact on our supporters.

What might you suggest we enhance at our organization? I've found this to be more useful than asking, "What can we do better?"

because it's open and comes from a perspective of *enhancing* rather than *fixing*. Once, a donor made a suggestion that simply hadn't occurred to me—that we make our email signature text bigger and include our direct phone numbers, because, as an older person, she had a difficult time reading them and hated fishing around the website for contact information when she needed to reach us. The fundraising team shared an exasperated, "Oh, my gosh. . ." because it was such a simple, useful, and logical thing for us to have done—but hadn't.

What might make the time you spend with our organization more meaningful? I can't tell you the number of times I've learned that a donor was a great fit to serve as a volunteer or board member after asking this question. While you might hear, "Nothing, it's all great," often the responses can be surprising and even powerful. One important caveat: make sure you have a response ready for donors who say, "I love writing you all a check once a year, but is there a way I might be more useful?" Some of them might be a good volunteer or board prospect, while others might enjoy serving as an organizational ambassador and sharing news and program highlights with others.

How do you prefer to be recognized? For organizations that are in the habit of raising up supporters, this is a really important question. Donors (people, companies, foundations, other institutions) give for myriad reasons, and while some are perfectly fine simply making a gift, others are grateful to have their name, logo, or likeness shared with the public. But please, if you do ask this question, be prepared to take careful note of the response. I once worked with an organization that was recognizing a husband and wife in print materials as "Mr. and Mrs. Smith"—only to realize later that the couple had different last names. As soon as the couple became aware of the mistake, they stopped giving, and that was that. The organization never followed up, and its silence spoke loudly.

Who do you see as our biggest competitor and/or potential collaborator/partner? This is a great question, though it should be asked of the right donor at the right time. By asking it, you can learn who your donors have on their radar when they survey the field, and it can also tell you where their support might go if, or when, they stop supporting your organization. You can then use that information to do an audit of your programs or other offerings to see how they compare and might be improved.

This content by the author originally appeared in Philanthropy News Digest *(December 2020).*

Bibliography

Allen, Madelyn-Burley. *Listening: The Forgotten Skill.* New York: Wiley, 1995.

Anderson, Virginia and Lauren Johnson. *Systems Thinking Basics: From Concepts to Causal Loops.* Massachusetts: Pegasus, 1997.

Baurain, Bradley. "Teaching, Listening, and Generative Silence." *Journal of Curriculum Theorizing* 27 no. 4 (2011) 89–101.

Beard, Alison. Interview with Art Markman and Kaitlin Woolley, HBR IdeaCast, podcast audio. December 07, 2021. https://hbr.org/podcast/2021/12/how-to-use-all-your-vacation-and-really-unplug.

Bloomerang. "A Guide to Donor Retention." https://bloomerang.co/blog/donor-retention.

Boyd, Steve. "The Beginning of Listening: Silence." SBoyd.com. 2005. https://sboyd.com/blog/articles/article-silence.

Brooks, David. "The Quest for Dignity." *The New York Times.* January 31, 2011. https://www.nytimes.com/2011/02/01/opinion/01brooks.html.

Building Movement Project. "Nonprofit Executives and the Racial Leadership Gap: A Race to Lead Brief." 2019. https://buildingmovement.org/wp-content/uploads/2019/07/Nonprofit-Executives-and-the-Racial-Leadership-Gap-Race-to-Lead-Brief.pdf.

Bureau of Labor Statistics. "Occupational Outlook Handbook." https://www.bls.gov/ooh/a-z-index.htm.

———. "Occupational Outlook Handbook: Fundraisers." https://www.bls.gov/ooh/business-and-financial/fundraisers.htm.

Burkhardt, John C. and Larry C. Spears. *Servant-Leadership and Philanthropic Institutions.* Indiana: The Greenleaf Center for Servant-Leadership, 2000.

Burton, Birgit Smith. "The Issue of Racism in the Fundraising Profession." Association of Fundraising Professionals. February 3, 2020. https://afpglobal.org/issue-racism-fundraising-profession.

Cascone, Sarah. "By Redeploying Her Staff in Some Ingenious New Ways, the Director of Texas's Blanton Museum Has Managed to Avoid Job Cuts Entirely." Artnet. May 27, 2020. https://news.artnet.com/art-world/how-blanton-museum-avoided-layoffs-1871334.

BIBLIOGRAPHY

Concord Leadership Group. "The Wakeup Call: A Study of Nonprofit Leadership in the US and Its Impending Crisis." 2018. https://concordleadershipgroup.com/report.

Davis, Paul and Larry C Spears. *Fortuitous Encounters: Wisdom Stories for Learning and Growth*. New Jersey: Paulist, 2013.

DeSalles, Marisa and Michelle Vryn. "The Annual Report That Never Was." Community-Centric Fundraising. November 24, 2021. https://communitycentricfundraising.org/2021/11/24/the-annual-report-that-never-was.

Duke, Annie. "3 Ways to Prepare for a Future You Can't Predict." Medium. June 8, 2020. https://marker.medium.com/3-ways-to-prepare-for-a-future-you-cant-predict-e34652b44169.

Ebarb, Tracy. "Nonprofits Fail—Here's Seven Reasons Why." Inside Charity. https://insidecharity.org/2019/09/07/nonprofits-fail-heres-seven-reasons-why-tracy-ebarb.

Eckels, Kaylene. "How Servant Leadership Supports Diversity in the Workplace." Etech. May 30, 2018. https://www.etechgs.com/blog/servant-leadership-supports-diversity-workplace.

EMERGE. "Post-Secondary Success Collaborative." https://www.emergefellowship.org/postsecondarycollaborative.

Falotico, Pat. "Servant-Leader: Why the Dash?" Robert K. Greenleaf Center for Servant Leadership. March 20, 2020. https://www.greenleaf.org/servant-leader-dash.

Ferch, Shann Ray, Larry C. Spears, Mary McFaland, and Michael R. Carey. *Conversations on Servant-Leadership: Insights on Human Courage in LIfe and Work*. New York: SUNY Press, 2015.

Fidelity Charitable. "The Role of Volunteering in Philanthropy" November 2020. https://www.fidelitycharitable.org/content/dam/fc-public/docs/resources/the-role-of-volunteering-in-philanthropy.pdf.

Follett, Mary Parker. *Creative Experience*. New York: Green and Co, 1924.

Fosslien, Liz and Mollie West Duffy. *No Hard Feelings: The Secret Power of Embracing Emotions at Work*. New York: Penguin, 2019.

Frick, Don M. *Greenleaf and Servant-Leader Listening*. Indiana: The Greenleaf Center for Servant-Leadership, 2011.

Fuller, Kristen. "The Difference Between Hearing and Listening." Psychology Today. July 8, 2021. https://www.psychologytoday.com/us/blog/happiness-is-state-mind/202107/the-difference-between-hearing-and-listening.

Give.org. "Give.org Donor Trust Report 2022: Five-Year Review of Trust and Giving Attitudes." 2022. https://www.give.org/docs/default-source/donor-trust-library/donor_trust_report_2022_five_year_review.pdf.

Goldin, Claudia and Cecilia Rouse. "Orchestrating Impartiality: The Impact of 'Blind' Auditions on Female Musicians." American Economic Review. September 2000. https://gap.hks.harvard.edu/orchestrating-impartiality-impact-"blind"-auditions-female-musicians.

Greenleaf, Robert K. *Servant Leadership: A Journey into the Nature of Legitimate Power and Greatness*. New York: Paulist, 1997.

BIBLIOGRAPHY

———. *The Power of Servant Leadership*. California: Barrett-Koehler, 1998.

Haddad, Duke. "What Is The Fundraising Cycle?" NonProfit PRO. May 17, 2019. https://www.nonprofitpro.com/post/what-is-the-fundraising-cycle.

Horsman, John Henry. *Servant-Leaders in Training: Foundations of the Philosophy of Servant-Leadership*. Switzerland: Palgrave Macmillan, 2018.

Hunt, Vivian, Dennis Layton, and Sara Prince. "Diversity Matters." McKinsey & Company. February 2, 2015. https://www.mckinsey.com/~/media/mckinsey/business%20functions/people%20and%20organizational%20performance/our%20insights/why%20diversity%20matters/diversity%20matters.pdf.

Internal Revenue Service. "Charitable Contributions: Substantiation and Disclosure Requirements." March 2016. https://www.irs.gov/pub/irs-pdf/p1771.pdf.

Kellerman, Barbara. *The End of Leadership*. New York: HarperCollins, 2012.

Kesler, Songya. "Servant Leadership Shadows: Martyring & Caretaking." Medium. May 20, 2020. https://medium.com/@songyakesler/servant-leadership-shadows-martyring-caretaking-665876c8aabe.

King Jr., Martin Luther. "Where Do We Go From Here?" Stanford University. August 16, 1967. https://kinginstitute.stanford.edu/where-do-we-go-here.

Klotz, Anthony C. and Mark C. Bolino. "Do You Really Know Why Employees Leave Your Company?" July 31, 2019. https://hbr.org/2019/07/do-you-really-know-why-employees-leave-your-company.

Lasley, Paul. "Two Empty Seats." AAA. 2021. https://www.aaa.com/dontdrive distracted/articles/twoemptyseats.html.

Lilly Family School of Philanthropy. "Giving USA: Total U.S. charitable giving remained strong in 2021, reaching $484.85 billion." June 21, 2022. https://philanthropy.iupui.edu/news-events/news-item/giving-usa:—total-u.s.-charitable-giving-remained-strong-in-2021,-reaching-$484.85-billion.html?id=392.

Lively, David and Naveen Vinukonda. "Calculating the Cost of Losing High-Performing Fundraisers." *The Chronicle of Philanthropy*. June 7, 2021. https://www.philanthropy.com/article/calculating-the-cost-of-losing-high-performing-fundraisers.

Lorenzo, Rocio, Nicole Voigt, Miki Tsusaka, Matt Krentz, and Katie Abouzahr. "How Diverse Leadership Teams Boost Innovation." January 23, 2018. https://www.bcg.com/publications/2018/how-diverse-leadership-teams-boost-innovation.

Lysakowski, Linda. "Top 10 Qualities of a Successful Fundraiser." Bloomerang. July 24, 2014. https://bloomerang.co/blog/top-10-qualities-of-a-successful-fundraiser.

Maslow, Abraham. *The Psychology of Science: A Reconnaissance*. New York: Harper & Row, 1966.

McCarthy, Niall. "Americans Wasted 768 Million Vacation Days Last Year." *Forbes*. August 19, 2019. https://www.forbes.com/sites/niallmccarthy/2019

/08/19/americans-wasted-768-million-vacation-days-last-year-infographic
/?sh=198f7b86248c.

McClaren, Samantha. "5 Essential Traits for Fundraisers in 2021." LinkedIn. April 14, 2021. https://nonprofit.linkedin.com/blog/2021/04/5-essential-traits-for-fundraisers-in-2021.

National Association of Nonprofit Organizations & Executives. "The Nonprofit Sector is a Non-Growth Sector." https://nanoe.org/join-nanoe.

National Council of Nonprofits. "Community of Practice." December 16, 2021. https://www.councilofnonprofits.org/tools-resources/community-of-practice.

———. "Nonprofit Impact Matters: How America's Charitable Nonprofits Strengthen Communities and Improve Lives." 2019. https://www.nonprofitimpactmatters.org/site/assets/files/1/nonprofit-impact-matters-sept-2019-1.pdf.

Newhouse, Chelsea. "Covid-19 Jobs Update, December 2021." Johns Hopkins Center for Civil Society Studies. January 11, 2022. http://ccss.jhu.edu/december-2021-jobs.

Northouse, Peter G. *Leadership: Theory and Practice.* California: Sage, 2019.

Papandrea, Dawn. "56% of Americans Donated to Charity in 2021, at Average of $574." LendingTree. November 29, 2021. https://www.lendingtree.com/debt-consolidation/charitable-donations-survey-study/#mostleastcharitablemetrosintheUS.

Peck, M. Scott. *The Road Less Traveled: A New Psychology of Love, Traditional Values and Spiritual Growth.* New York: Simon & Schuster, 1978.

Pun, Elizabeth. "6 Key Skills of All-Star Development Professionals." Classy. July 20, 2015. https://www.classy.org/blog/6-key-skills-of-all-star-development-professionals.

Rice University. "Transportation Equity: The Time is Now." November 11, 2020. https://www.youtube.com/watch?v=W1hpWeJMqJo.

Rogers, Carl. *A Way of Being.* Boston: Houghton Mifflin, 1995.

Salamon, Lester and Chelsea Newhouse. "The 2020 Nonprofit Employment Report: Nonprofit Economic Data Bulletin no. 48." Johns Hopkins Center for Civil Society Studies. June 2020. http://ccss.jhu.edu/wp-content/uploads/downloads/2020/06/2020-Nonprofit-Employment-Report_FINAL_6.2020.pdf.

Senge, Peter M. *The Fifth Discipline: The Art and Practice of the Learning Organization.* New York: Penguin Random House, 1990.

Siebert, Rachel D'Souza. "Does Your Organization's Storytelling Perpetuate Harm?" Nonprofit Marketing Guide. February 9, 2022. https://www.nonprofitmarketingguide.com/does-your-organizations-storytelling-perpetuate-harm.

Siegel, Dan and Jenny Yancey. "Philanthropy's Forgotten Resource? Engaging the Individual Donor: The State of Donor Education Today & A Leadership Agenda for The Road Ahead." New visions Philanthropic Research &

Development. 2003. https://hewlett.org/wp-content/uploads/2016/08/ PhilanthropysForgottenResource.pdf.

Sipe, James W. and Don M. Frick. *Seven Pillars of Servant Leadership*. New Jersey: Paulist, 2015.

Spears, Larry C. "Character and servant leadership: Ten characteristics of effective, caring leaders." Regent University. 2010. https://www.regent.edu/ journal/journal-of-virtues-leadership/character-and-servant-leadership-ten-characteristics-of-effective-caring-leaders.

Statista. "Revenues of Reporting Nonprofit Organizations in the U.S. From 1998 to 2016." https://www.statista.com/statistics/189260/revenues-of-reporting-non-profit-organizations-in-the-us-since-1998.

Tax Policy Center. "How Did the TCJA Affect Incentives for Charitable Giving?" https://www.taxpolicycenter.org/briefing-book/how-did-tcja-affect-incentives-charitable-giving.

Urban Institute. "Nonprofit Trends and Impacts 2021: National Findings on Donation Trends from 2015 through 2020, Diversity and Representation, and First-Year Impacts of the COVID-19 Pandemic." October 2021. https://www.urban.org/sites/default/files/publication/104889/nonprofit-trends-and-impacts-2021_1_0.pdf.

Volpe, Rob. "5 Ways to Put Empathy to Work Right Now." Ignite360. https:// www.ignite-360.com/blog/5-ways-to-put-empathy-to-work-right-now.

Wagner, Lilya. "Fundraising, the CEO, and Servant Leadership." 2014. https:// documents.adventistarchives.org/conferences/Docs/2014Tertiary PresidentsConf/Fundraising%20and%20Servant%20Leadership.pdf.

Waltner-Pepper, Heidi. "10 Core Personality Traits of Effective Fundraisers." TWB Fundraising. April 23, 2018. https://blog.twbfundraising.com/key-qualities-of-a-fundraiser.

World Health Organization. "Burn-out an 'occupational phenomenon': International Classification of Diseases." May 19, 2019. https://www.who. int/news/item/28–05-2019-burn-out-an-occupational-phenomenon-international-classification-of-diseases.

Made in the USA
Columbia, SC
03 February 2024

31417247R00050